Experiencing GOD'S Power in Worship

Experiencing
GOD'S
Power
in Worship

Dr. David E. Fischer

Whitaker House

Unless otherwise indicated, all Scripture quotations are taken from the *New King James Version*, © 1979, 1980, 1982 by Thomas Nelson, Inc. Used by permission. All rights reserved.

Scripture quotations marked (KJV) are taken from the *King James Version* of the Bible.

Scripture quotations marked (NIV) are from the Holy Bible, *New International Version*, © 1973, 1978, 1984 by the International Bible Society. Used by permission.

EXPERIENCING GOD'S POWER IN WORSHIP

Dr. David Fischer
Living Waters Christian Fellowship
2495 E. Mountain Street
Pasadena, CA 91104
Tel: 626-791-7295; FAX: 626-791-7634
www.livingwaters.org
FischLine@aol.com

ISBN: 0-88368-552-3
Printed in the United States of America
Copyright © 1998 by Whitaker House

Whitaker House
30 Hunt Valley Circle
New Kensington, PA 15068

Library of Congress Cataloging-in-Publication Data

Fischer, David, 1938–
    Experiencing God's power in worship / by David Fischer.
        p.   cm.
    Includes bibliographical references.
    ISBN 0-88368-552-3 (trade paper)
    1. God—Worship and love. I. Title.
BV4817.F47 1998
248.3—dc21   98-44454

Contents

Dedication

My wife, Elaine, provided me with constant encouragement and faith in this project, which helped me to complete the manuscript. Her feedback and insight concerning the contents of the book were very valuable.

The Senior Pastors of my church, Willard and Ione Glaeser, were used of the Lord to birth in my heart and spirit much of the revelation reflected in the contents of this book. They are both with the Lord now, but their ministry continues to have a great effect.

Finally, I owe much to Rev. Charlotte Baker, who in the formative years of my understanding of praise and worship, was used by God to communicate much truth to my mind and much passion to my spirit concerning ministry to the Lord.

Chapter 1

The Power and Glory of Heaven

Your will be done on earth as it is in heaven.
—Matthew 6:10

The glorious personage of the Son of Man sits upon His throne; light radiates from His face *"like the sun shining in all its brilliance"* (Rev. 1:16 NIV). Celestial light and glory stream everywhere like rays of the sun.

Around the throne, circling rank upon rank, column upon column, angels, hundreds of millions of them—and millions more—spiral majestically like soaring eagles in the heavens. They hover near the throne, catching the light and glory streaming from the One seated there, reflecting this glory onto the faces of the creatures surrounding the throne. They also move far, far away, stretching into the dimensions of the heavens as far as the eye can see. Angels suspended in shimmering beams of glory stream out from the throne, circling in rows and ranks. Their wings catch glints of glory in the far reaches of the heavens, reflecting that glory along the path from which it came.

Millions and millions of angels shimmer in the rays of glory while the whole panoply of light rotates and swirls, yet not against darkness. Glory upon glory and light upon light stream from the throne as the source.

Swirling banks of angels move majestically with the sound of worship. Sometimes they are stationary while sustained tones of praise and worship pour forth from them to the One seated upon the throne. Sometimes they move, circling the throne like giant spokes of celestial wheels, moving through swaths of glory with glinting wings, flashing through the heavens as powerful waves of praise and worship surround the One seated there.

9

Experiencing God's Power in Worship

EARTHLY WORSHIP

The glorious worship of heaven is so far removed from its counterpart on earth. What a contrast it makes with the monotonous drone of bored, lazy singing, as parishioners yawn their way through centuries-old tunes, while over their heads in the heavens, the splendor and glory of the God of all creation is being extolled continuously in magnificent displays of beauty and sound.

What a paradox our worship services are when viewed from God's perspective! He looks upon our churches across the earth and hears His people praying every Sunday, *"Your will be done on earth as it is in heaven."* No wonder He taught us to pray that way, for what is happening on earth in the realms of worship and praise is certainly not what is being done in heaven. Instead of the thundering power and life-giving joy of the praise of heaven, we often discover just the opposite here on earth: cold, dead religion.

God desires with all His heart for our worship experiences here on earth to be marked by the same creativity, power, and release as is true of heavenly worship. By the Spirit, He even brought one man into heaven itself to catch a glimpse of the glorious worship there and to tell us what he saw, as if to whet our appetites for such an experience of true worship here on earth and to spark our faith to believe and pray for so much more. The apostle John described for us what he saw and heard: *"Worthy is the Lamb who was slain!"* (Rev. 5:12).

PROPHETIC REVELATIONS OF WORSHIP

That cry resounded through the heavens as if rippling on the surface of unseen waters, as wave after wave of sound echoed from the voices of hundreds of millions of angels: *"To receive power!"* (v. 12). The words rose in volume, carried by the loud voices of all the ranks of angels and creatures, reaching the farthest limits of heaven. *"And riches"* (v. 12). Echoes of sound reverberated through the heavens, continuing with these words: *"And wisdom" "and strength" "and honor" "and glory" "and blessing!"* (v. 12).

The prophet Isaiah saw the same thing in the Spirit:

I saw the Lord sitting on a throne, high and lifted up, and the train of His robe filled the temple. Above it stood seraphim; each one had six wings: with two he covered his face, with two he covered his feet, and with two he flew. And one cried to another and said: "Holy, holy, holy is the LORD of hosts; the whole earth is full of His glory!"

(Isa. 6:1–3)

"*Holy, holy, holy.*" Hallelujah, hallelujah, hallelujah! The worship of the Lamb upon the throne eclipses the most glorious light and music spectacles of earth! It exceeds the glory of a million "Hallelujah" choruses! It outshines the beauty of all the earthly celebrations ever imagined!

SILENCE VERSUS SYMPHONIC PRAISE

God desires worship to be the most exhilarating and fulfilling experience of our relationship with Him as our beings are filled with the wonder of His presence. Yet how far short we fall of His desire for our worship, how far *"short of the glory of God"* (Rom. 3:23).

Nowhere is the disparity between heaven and earth—the distance between the mighty, powerful praise and worship of heaven and the coldness and lethargy of worship services on earth—more clearly seen than in the volume and intensity of the sound of the worship itself. The mighty thundering of sound heard in the heavens far surpasses the weakness of the volume of singing often heard, or barely heard, in church services today!

Signs in church foyers read, "Worship service in progress. Silence, please." And we are so fond of the Scripture, *"The LORD is in His holy temple. Let all earth keep silence before Him"* (Hab. 2:20). Yet from the context, the truth emerges that it is the heathen voices, the clamoring and mocking cries of the nations, that are to be silenced, so that God can roar out of Zion, His people! The psalmist David cried out:

You have turned for me my mourning into dancing; You have put off my sackcloth and clothed me with gladness, to

the end that my glory may sing praise to You and not be silent. O LORD my God, I will give thanks to You forever.
(Ps. 30:11–12)

There are some who don't praise the Lord: *"The dead do not praise the LORD, nor any who go down into silence. But we will bless the LORD from this time forth and forevermore"* (Ps. 115:17–18).

WHEN EARTHLY PRAISE TURNED HEAVENLY

In Bible times, the mighty power of God impacted His people on earth, and the same intensity and volume of worship occurred *"as it is in heaven."* The presence of the Creator elicits from all His creation the most powerful responses of joy in shouts of praise and great volumes of worship.

On the Day of Pentecost, when the church was born, *"there came a sound from heaven, as of a rushing mighty wind"* (Acts 2:2), which was mingled with the praises of the disciples and sounded forth with such power that *"the multitude came together"* (v. 6), a crowd so large that *"about three thousand souls"* (v. 41) were born again.

At other times in Israel's history, the power of worship and praise also thundered out of God's people. In the days of Ezra, when the Jews returned from Babylon to Jerusalem and rebuilt the temple of the Lord,

All the people shouted with a great shout, when they praised the LORD....Many of the priests...wept with a loud voice....Many shouted aloud for joy, so that the people could not discern the noise of the shout of joy from the noise of the weeping of the people, for the people shouted with a loud shout, and the sound was heard afar off.
(Ezra 3:11–13)

In Nehemiah's day, when the great wall of Jerusalem was finally completed, the joy of the city was heard at a great distance:

Also that day they offered great sacrifices, and rejoiced, for God had made them rejoice with great joy; the women and

the children also rejoiced, so that the joy of Jerusalem was heard afar off. (Neh. 12:43)

At the coronation of King Solomon, the shouts of praise of the city of Jerusalem were so intense that the earth split open!

And they blew the trumpet; and all the people said, God save king Solomon. And all the people came up after him, and the people piped with pipes, and rejoiced with great joy, so that the earth rent with the sound of them.

(1 Kings 1:39–40 KJV)

The meaning of the Hebrew word for *rent* is clear: "to cleave, break, rip, or open." Solomon's enemies, miles away, heard the sound and cried out, *"Why is the city in such a noisy uproar?"* (v. 41).

There are other accounts in Scripture of the intensity of praise and worship when the power of God is present among His people. True praise and worship here on earth as it is being done in heaven is full of life, intensity, and reverberating sound! And when we are praying for the will of God to be done *"on earth as it is in heaven,"* we are praying for the divine impact of the presence of God upon us, which produces the same magnificent expression of sound as is now being heard around the throne of God in heaven.

CELESTIAL SOUNDS OF WORSHIP

It is this powerful sound of praise and worship in the heavens that so distinguishes celestial worship from its earthly counterpart. As the voice of God shook the earth at Mount Sinai (Heb. 12:26), imagine the voices of a hundred million angels and millions more—*"ten thousand times ten thousand, and thousands of thousands"* (Rev. 5:11)—all praising God with a *"loud voice"* (v. 12).

Oh, the sound of heaven! Swirling waves of worship radiate in all dimensions and directions. Millions of harpists and worshipers crescendo like thousands of thundering waterfalls. The source of the sound moving in the heavens comes from the circling host of angels rotating around the throne—producing

13

three dimensional sound. Rank upon rank of the angelic hosts move and worship, move and worship, creating rotating orbs of celestial praise to the One seated upon the throne.

> *Then the Spirit lifted me up, and I heard behind me a great thunderous voice: "Blessed is the glory of the LORD from His place!" I also heard the noise of the wings of the living creatures that touched [kissed] one another, and the noise of the wheels beside them, and a great thunderous noise.* (Ezek. 3:12–13)

> *And He rode upon a cherub, and flew; He flew upon the wings of the wind.* (Ps. 18:10)

> *When they went, I heard the noise of their wings, like the noise of many waters, like the voice of the Almighty, a tumult like the noise of an army.* (Ezek. 1:24)

The *"noise of many waters"* is the sound of heaven. It is produced by rivers of praise and worship, which pour forth from all the creatures and angels and the redeemed in the heavenlies; it is the corporate voice of the Lord expressed through all His creatures, the glorious sound of hundreds of millions of voices raised in worship.

> *And I heard a voice from heaven, like the voice of many waters, and like the voice of loud thunder. And I heard the sound of harpists playing their harps.* (Rev. 14:2)

> *I heard a loud voice of a great multitude in heaven, saying, "Alleluia! Salvation and glory and honor and power belong to the Lord our God!"* (Rev. 19:1)

> *And I heard, as it were, the voice of a great multitude, as the sound of many waters and as the sound of mighty thunderings, saying, "Alleluia! For the Lord God Omnipotent reigns!"* (v. 6)

THE SOURCE OF WORSHIP

The voice of the Lord, the voice of the Almighty Himself, becomes the corporate voice of all His creatures raised in praise.

14

John said of Jesus, *"His voice was like the sound of rushing waters"* (Rev. 1:15 NIV). It is as if the Spirit of the Lord Himself flowing through the myriads of worshipers becomes their voices, and their voices become His! It is a glorious entanglement and interweaving of beings, a divine fellowship, an intercommunion among worshipers and their Lord, more intimate and more glorious than any fellowship on earth could ever be.

This is the awesome and majestic mystery of God Himself. He encompasses all things and yet is over and above all, imminently present and yet transcendently glorified, high and lifted up and yet very present and very near, receiving the worship of millions of beings and yet at the same time is the very source of all their worship by the Spirit. He receives all of them together as one, yet relates personally with each one separately, as if each one stood alone at His throne in loving adoration, a personal individuality of direct relationship with the One upon the throne with awareness, recognition, and love flowing between them. Yet everyone is grandly aware of the millions of fellow worshipers surrounding the throne together, as myriads of beings create the magnificent crescendos of worship in the heavens; together, yet one, each one needs the others to extend the glorious harmonies and swelling praises to the limits of music and speech.

Millions upon millions of worshiping creatures and praisers relate personally to the One seated upon the throne. It is as if the glory streaming from His face is reflected on Him from each angel and each individual as a personal resonance, a personal relationship of love. The very presence of the One who created them evokes a response of love and worship: *"Deep calls unto deep"* (Ps. 42:7); the sons of God shout for joy (Job 38:7).

THE CELESTIAL GLORY OF THE ALMIGHTY GOD

How drab earthly worship is when compared with the beauty of heavenly worship. What talents and creative gifts lie dormant in our churches that could be displaying the beauty and glory of God in color, sound, and movement in our sanctuaries. Our earthly worship services seem lackluster in comparison to the brilliance of heaven. What glory shines there! The colors radiate in their purity. They are crystal clear, not opaque and diffuse as if tinged with earthly impurities, but deep and transparent.

The Son of Man Himself was like jasper and carnelian to look on, seated upon a throne of sapphire. Covering the whole magnificently glorious scene was an emerald rainbow (Rev. 4:2–3), sparkling, shining, and emanating its glory to blend with the brilliant golden amber of the burning fire, which surrounded the Son of Man (v. 5).

> *And above...was the likeness of a throne, in appearance like a sapphire stone; on the likeness of the throne was a likeness with the appearance of a man high above it....I saw...the color of amber with the appearance of fire all around within it; and from the appearance of His waist and downward I saw, as it were, the appearance of fire with brightness all around. Like the appearance of a rainbow in a cloud on a rainy day, so was the appearance of the brightness all around it. This was the appearance of the likeness of the glory of the LORD. So when I saw it, I fell on my face.* (Ezek. 1:26–28)

"Seven lamps of fire were burning before the throne, which are the seven Spirits of God" (Rev. 4:5). They cast their light upon all the worship and movement surrounding the glorious throne of the Lord. And the sea of glass, that crystal sea, stretched out from the throne, highlighted with flashing flames of fire that fell into the earth beneath (Rev. 15:2; 16:8), a pure, transparent crystal ocean or *"firmament"* (Ezek. 1:22). Ezekiel saw the worshiping creatures on earth standing under this crystal sea, which he called a *"firmament."* It was *"like the color of an awesome crystal, stretched out over their heads"* (v. 22). He also described what was going on in heaven above this crystal sea. *"Above the firmament over their heads"* was the throne of God in the heavenlies (v. 26).

This crystal firmament, then, was the separation or barrier between heaven and earth, between time and eternity, between the realm of the Spirit and that of flesh and blood. The firmament overlays everything. Above it was the heavenly realm, the eternal glory, the abode of the Holy One and His throne of judgment.

From above, it is almost as if one can see through this crystal firmament into the affairs of men on earth. It is as if openings could be made in the firmament, and fire and water could be poured out upon the earth; but men on earth cannot see back up through it, not having eyes of the Spirit or the spiritual ability to ascend through the firmament into the heavenly realm. Yet the apostle John was taken *"up"* (Rev. 4:1) *"in the Spirit on the Lord's Day"* (Rev. 1:10) through a *"door"* (Rev. 4:1) into this realm of heaven and has communicated to us what he saw using the limited words of human vocabulary:

I was in the Spirit on the Lord's Day, and I heard behind me a loud voice, as of a trumpet....After these things I looked, and behold, a door standing open in heaven. And the first voice which I heard was like a trumpet speaking with me, saying, "Come up here."...Immediately I was in the Spirit; and behold, a throne set in heaven, and One sat on the throne. And He who sat there was like a jasper and a sardius stone in appearance; and there was a rainbow around the throne, in appearance like an emerald....And from the throne proceeded lightnings, thunderings, and voices. Seven lamps of fire were burning before the throne, which are the seven Spirits of God. Before the throne there was a sea of glass, like crystal. (Rev. 1:10; 4:1–3, 5–6)

Then I looked, and I heard the voice of many angels around the throne, the living creatures, and the elders; and the number of them was ten thousand times ten thousand, and thousands of thousands, saying with a loud voice: "Worthy is the Lamb who was slain to receive power and riches and wisdom, and strength and honor and glory and blessing!" And every creature which is in heaven and on the earth and under the earth and such as are in the sea, and all that are in them, I heard saying: "Blessing and honor and glory and power be to Him who sits on the throne, and to the Lamb, forever and ever!" Then the four living creatures said, "Amen!" And the twenty-four elders fell down and worshiped Him who lives forever and ever.
(Rev. 5:11–14)

Then a voice came from the throne, saying, "Praise our God, all you His servants and those who fear Him, both

17

> *small and great!" And I heard, as it were, the voice of a*
> *great multitude, as the sound of many waters and as the*
> *sound of mighty thunderings, saying, "Alleluia! For the*
> *Lord God Omnipotent reigns!"* (Rev. 19:5–6)

Such is the splendor and glory of heaven's worship. Seemingly so far removed from earth, so remote, this overwhelming glory and power of the worship of heaven has actually burst forth in some very notable occasions on earth, as recorded for us in Scripture. Through the eyes of biblical writers, let us see descriptions of what has already happened here on earth. Perhaps we will be able to see enough to realize, at least in a measure, what we are praying for when we say, *"Your will be done on earth as it is in heaven."*

Chapter 2

Glimpses of Heaven on Earth

a few instances are recorded in Scripture when the celestial glory of God broke through the crystal firmament that separates heaven from earth. The glory was actually seen in the realm of time and space. A few times, the glory of God appeared to men when they caught glimpses of heaven on earth.

We used to walk continuously in the light and glory of His countenance; the glory of God used to clothe us in garments of light. Adam and his wife fellowshiped with God daily when they heard His prophetic voice, the manifestation of His presence, as He walked in the Garden *"in the cool* [or wind] *of the day"* (Gen. 3:8). The very Spirit of God moved upon them, and the Word of the Lord spoke directly with them. Then came the awful tragedy of sin.

THE VEIL OF DEATH

Since that dreadful day when sin entered human life, all have fallen *"short of the glory of God"* (Rom. 3:23). There has been a lifting up from the earth of God's manifest presence, and a flaming sword now bars men from the Tree of Life (Gen. 3:24). Instead of an open heaven and direct communion with the Father, the veil of death is now spread out over all the nations of the earth, covering the eyes of men and blinding them to the heavenly realm and its glory (Isa. 25:7). *"The god of this world hath blinded the minds of them which believe not, lest the light of the glorious gospel of Christ...should shine unto them"* (2 Cor. 4:4 KJV).

Since the expulsion from the Garden of Eden until Christ would pierce this veil by His death and resurrection, the glory of God would remain hidden to the eyes of men—except for some very notable exceptions.

MOSES BEHIND THE VEIL

God appeared in His glory to the man who had first seen that glory in the fire of the burning bush. The Lord God Jehovah called His servant Moses up into His presence on the top of Mount Sinai. Only this man enjoyed the presence of God, while the rest of the nation remained in darkness. The people of Israel saw only the underside of the awesome cloud that covered or veiled the glory of God from their sight. They shrunk back in fear and terror as smoking blackness descended upon the mountaintop.

Thunder shook the landscape. Bolts of lightning flashed out of the black billows as the mountain was transformed before their eyes into a smoking blast furnace. Fire, rumblings, earthquakes, and the awesome tone of a trumpet pierced the silence, growing louder and louder, enough to shatter the ears.

> *Mount Sinai was completely in smoke, because the LORD descended upon it in fire. Its smoke ascended like the smoke of a furnace, and the whole mountain quaked greatly.* (Exod. 19:18)

> *There were thunderings and lightnings, and a thick cloud on the mountain; and the sound of the trumpet was very loud.* (v. 16)

It was dreadful. It was like a firestorm, a tempest with tremendous force and power. None dared to go near (Exod. 20:18). "You go for us, Moses," they cried. "Tell us what God has said. We cannot bear to hear Him ourselves, for we will all die!" (v. 19). Moses exhorted, *"'Do not fear; for God has come to test you, and that His fear may be before you, so that you may not sin.' But I am going up to meet with Him"* (v. 20). As the people watched from afar, cringing and trembling in fear, *"Moses drew near the thick darkness where God was"* (v. 21).

GOD IS A MYSTERY

In a similar way, Christians, today, are content to let their pastor or worship leader penetrate into the awesomeness of God's presence, but they shrink back from entering in themselves. Are they afraid of the unknown, fearful of encountering the living God? Are they unwilling to expend the energy necessary to diligently seek Him? Many modern saints wonder why God isn't more easily accessible. Why can't He appear as quickly and effortlessly as the picture on a TV screen? In spite of our well-spelled-out doctrines and our answers to all possible questions, although we are buttressed with dozens of Bible references and have heard the truth expounded in thousands of tapes and conferences, the simple, unalterable fact remains: what a mystery God is! The apostle Paul declared, *"And without controversy great is the mystery of godliness"* (1 Tim. 3:16).

He hides light with darkness, conceals glory with judgment. He covers love with fear, veils His glory with the storm. What a mystery our God is! He hides Himself from all and then chooses those to whom He will reveal Himself out of His hiddenness and calls them to Himself. *"Truly You are God, who hide[s] Yourself, O God of Israel, the Savior!"* (Isa. 45:15). *"No one knows who the Son is except the Father, and who the Father is except the Son, and the one to whom the Son wills to reveal Him"* (Luke 10:22).

MOSES IN GOD'S PRESENCE

As Moses rose higher and higher up the fearful and foreboding mountain, the people watched him slowly disappear from sight into the blackness, the tempest, the firestorm. Up, up, up he went, and suddenly, he broke through! As an Alpine climber emerges above the clouds into a bright sky, Moses surfaced above the billows—no longer black and foreboding, but glorious and glistening white as the glory of the light was reflected off them. No more lightnings and thunderings and fire were seen or heard. He had left them behind in the valley below. Now, only peace and glory remained.

He bowed the heavens also, and came down with darkness under His feet....His canopy around Him was dark waters and thick clouds of the skies. From the brightness before Him, His thick clouds passed. (Ps. 18:9, 11–12)

With clouds he covereth the light; and commandeth it not to shine by the cloud that cometh betwixt. (Job 36:32 KJV)

Can any understand the spreadings of the clouds? ...Behold, he spreadeth his light upon it. (vv. 29–30 KJV)

And now men see not the bright light which is in the clouds. (Job 37:21 KJV)

Moses saw that light, the glory of God reflected off the clouds below. Only the light of His presence shone. Heaven had come to earth! The underside of the clouds of God had been awesome and fearful because of sin. But Moses was above them now, in the glory, light, and love of God, miraculously preserved without food or drink for forty days and forty nights—living in His presence.

At the end of his life Moses could reflect upon that glorious experience, speaking of the tens of thousands of angelic hosts that attended the presence of the Lord upon the mountaintop. Thousands upon thousands of angels, rank upon rank of saints, or sanctified ones, who lived in the glory of the Lord, circled in the heavens as the light of heaven was for a brief moment in time manifest upon the mountaintop of Sinai. Ablaze with glory, this earthly manifestation of the heavenly realm was attended by thousands of heavenly hosts:

The LORD came from Sinai...and He came with ten thousands of saints; from His right hand came a fiery law for them. Yes, He loves the people; all His saints are in Your hand; they sit down at Your feet; everyone receives Your words. (Deut. 33:2–3)

MOSES REVEALS GOD'S LOVE

Moses spoke of the love God had for His people, the love manifest above the black clouds of judgment and the fiery law, the love that Moses himself experienced upon the mountaintop. *"Yes, He loves the people."* Moses experienced a glorious communion with the Father as he sat peacefully at His feet and received His words—forty days and nights of wonderful teaching, chapters of intimate details about the moral law of God and the construction of the tabernacle. *"They sit down at Your feet."* Moses could only describe the marvelous receiving of the Word of the Lord into his heart and mind as the gentle distilling of the rain and the dew upon the earth.

A glorious revelation awaits those of us today who, like Moses, have been lifted by grace beyond the rumblings of godly fear and judgment and have scaled the mountain of the Lord to bask in His glorious light and receive His implanted Word into our hearts. No longer do the thundering trumpet tones of impending judgment shake the earth and set the mountains trembling, but high above the rumblings of judgment echoing in the valley below, the love-implanted words of God are received deep into the soul. Moses spoke of this kind of revelation that he experienced on Mount Sinai:

> *Give ear, O heavens, and I will speak; and hear, O earth, the words of my mouth. Let my teaching drop as the rain, my speech distill as the dew, as raindrops on the tender herb, and as showers on the grass.* (Deut. 32:1–2)

The Radiance of God

And then, almost as suddenly as it had come, God and His glory lifted off the mountaintop. Only His hiddenness remained, leaving behind the only vestige of God's presence that lingered. The glory and radiance upon Moses' face, the afterglow of the power of the heavenly realm that had preserved Moses for forty days and nights, were still to be seen. And even that glory had to be hidden. It had to be shielded from the view of sinful men by the veil or covering that Moses put upon his face, just as the glory of God had to be hidden by the clouds upon the mountain. Men could not look upon it and live.

> *So when Aaron and all the children of Israel saw Moses, behold, the skin of his face shone, and they were afraid to come near him.* (Exod. 34:30)

23

And when Moses had finished speaking with them, he put a veil on his face. But whenever Moses went in before the LORD to speak with Him, he would take the veil off until he came out. (vv. 33–34)

THE HIDDEN GLORY

Moses built the tabernacle according to the blueprint that the Lord gave him on Mount Sinai, and it also had a veil. Behind the veil, on which were embroidered the figures of cherubim, symbolic of heaven, was the gloriously dreadful and awesome room, the Holy of Holies, in which was placed the golden ark of the covenant.

Upon the ark of the covenant rested the glory of God, once again hidden from the view of Israel and visible only once a year to one man, the high priest, who entered behind the veil for a brief moment to ceremonially offer blood and incense before the Lord. The rest of Israel stood outside, unable to view the manifestation of the glory of God. They gazed from afar at the awesome pillar of cloud and fire that hovered above the tabernacle, pointing downward toward the Holy of Holies. On Mount Sinai, that cloud had also concealed the glory of God from them. The glory remained hidden now once again within the Holy of Holies. The Holy of Holies was hidden within the tabernacle, and the tabernacle was hidden within the linen curtains of the courtyard.

After the sin of Israel in the idolatrous worship of the golden calf, the glory of God became even more remote. Moses moved the tabernacle out of the center of the camp to its outer perimeter, and the people had to view the pillar of cloud and fire from an even greater distance:

Moses took his tent and pitched it outside the camp, far from the camp....When Moses entered the tabernacle,...the pillar of cloud descended and stood at the door of the tabernacle....All the people saw the pillar of cloud standing at the tabernacle door, and all the people rose and worshiped, each man in his tent door. (Exod. 33:7, 9–10)

Such was the posture of Israel during most of its history: standing, waiting, and watching from afar—wondering, maybe at times seeking after the glory of God, yet unable to actually touch and experience it. Indeed, such has been the plight of all mankind: unable to see the glory of God, unable to find rest at His throne, unable to see His kingdom. No wonder Jesus cried out, *"Unless one is born again, he cannot see the kingdom of God"* (John 3:3). And to be sure, before Christ came, during the history of the Old Testament people, the glimpses of the glory of God were rare.

THE GLORIOUS ANNOUNCEMENT

Except for scattered times of true revival in Israel when the manifest glory and presence of God moved among them in response to their worship, all that remained for Israel were encounters at a distance. On rare occasions, the prophets of old glimpsed the glory of the Son of Man with His eyes like lamps of fire, His face like lightning, and His voice like the sound of a multitude (Dan. 10:6). They had to view the external covering of the glory, following from afar, until that day on the Judean hillside when the glory of God burst forth upon this earth once again. This time the most revolutionary declaration was announced to man:

> *Do not be afraid, for behold, I bring you good tidings of great joy which will be to all people. For there is born to you this day in the City of David a Savior, who is Christ the Lord.* (Luke 2:10–11)

To you is born a Savior, to all people, a Savior, to the whole world, a Savior. The Christ, the Anointed One who was to come, the Messiah has come!

Heaven could not restrain itself! The firmament parted—that separation between heaven and earth. Countless numbers of angelic hosts poured out into view of the shepherds that night. First the glory of God shone around them. Then they looked up in amazement as the voice of a single angel proclaimed the Savior's birth. And then the hosts of heaven began appearing. Rank upon rank, swirling and spiraling as on eagles' wings in the brilliant glory of the heavens, their wings flashed in the light. The praises of the Almighty filled the heavens that night as *"Glory to God in the highest, and on earth peace, good-will toward men!"* (v. 14) reverberated through the atmosphere and echoed off the Judean hills.

As suddenly as it had begun, it was over. The angels vanished into the heavens from which they had come, and the shepherds were left with the awesome memory of a heavenly visitation and the strange announcement of the birth of a baby in the city of Bethlehem.

THE ONE WHO BRINGS TRUE WORSHIP

One thing, at least, was clear. The revelation of the heavenly kingdom and its worship was somehow linked to this mysterious babe in Bethlehem. In order to learn more about the glories of heaven, we would need to know more about Him. In order to enter into the true worship of heaven, it would have to be through Him. In order to come to the Father, it would have to be through Him. Jesus said to Thomas, *"I am the way, the truth, and the life. No man comes to the Father except through Me"* (John 14:6).

Chapter 3

Heaven and Earth United in Christ

*C*hrist is our Mediator. He is the bridge between heaven and earth, the ladder that Jacob saw with its foot on earth and its top in heaven. Christ is the door into paradise. He is the One who came to destroy sin and death, to open the door into glory for all mankind who believe!

Christ, through His atoning death on the cross and His shed blood, has opened the way boldly through the veil that once concealed the glory of God from us. He has led us into the throne room of heaven, into the Holy of Holies, into the glory of God and fellowship with the Father.

> *Having boldness to enter the Holiest by the blood of Jesus, by a new and living way which He consecrated for us, through the veil, that is, His flesh...let us draw near with a true heart.* (Heb. 10:19–20, 22)

The veil has been pierced forever. That veil that had hidden the glory of God from men is now gone. Jesus, our eternal High Priest, entered once for all time into heaven with His own blood to make permanent atonement for us all.

He died, rose again, and ascended into the glory of heaven to open a way for us now to pass *"within the veil"* (Heb. 6:19 KJV), directly into the presence of God, even before His throne, by the Spirit.

> *Seeing then that we have a great High Priest who has passed through the heavens, Jesus the Son of God....Let us*

therefore come boldly to the throne of grace, that we may obtain mercy and find grace to help in time of need.

(Heb. 4:14, 16)

THE TORN VEIL

As if to show the world that by the death of His Son on Calvary the separation between heaven and earth had been removed, allowing men to enter into the very presence of God, the Father Himself took hold of the natural veil in the Temple of Herod, which had withheld His glory from men by permanently concealing it in the Holy of Holies. As Jesus cried on the cross of Calvary, *"It is finished!"* (John 19:30), God ripped that veil apart from top to bottom: *"And Jesus cried out with a loud voice, and breathed His last. Then the veil of the temple was torn in two from top to bottom"* (Mark 15:37–38).

Jesus then died and passed into Hades, releasing the men and women of faith of all ages from the chains of death. Then as He burst forth from the tomb in His glorious Resurrection, raised from death by the power and Spirit of holiness, He ascended into heaven itself to sit upon the throne of His Father. This was not simply the triumph of a single individual, not just a single perfect example of victory, remote from us and known only by doctrinal revelation and theological distance.

The death, resurrection, and ascension of Jesus Christ has marvelously affected mankind for all time and for eternity. A cosmic change was wrought behind the scenes in the unseen realms of the heavenlies. Jesus opened paradise to men of faith. *"Today you will be with Me in Paradise,"* He told the thief on the cross who believed in Him (Luke 23:43). Behind the cross and the tomb, Jesus was opening heaven's gates to redeemed mankind. Unseen by mortal men, a door to paradise was opened in the heavens *"through the veil"* (Heb. 10:20) into the very presence of God the Father. Eternal fellowship was now restored between God and man.

That which was from the beginning...that eternal life which was with the Father and was manifested to us...we declare to you, that you also may have fellowship with us;

and truly our fellowship is with the Father and with His Son Jesus Christ. (1 John 1:1–3)

And this is eternal life, that they may know You, the only true God, and Jesus Christ whom You have sent.
(John 17:3)

THE FEAR OF DEATH

Before Calvary, when faithful men died, it meant confinement in the shadowy regions of *Sheol* (Hebrew) or *Hades* (Greek), the place of departed souls in the *"lower parts of the earth"* (Ps. 63:9). For the saints in Old Testament times, the prospect of dying must have been a fearful and terrifying experience from which their souls recoiled in horror. King Hezekiah cried out in joyful relief after his life was spared:

Thou hast in love to my soul delivered it from the pit of corruption....For the grave cannot praise thee, death can not celebrate thee: they that go down into the pit cannot hope for thy truth. (Isa. 38:17–18 KJV)

And the psalmist cried out, *"The dead do not praise the LORD, nor any who go down into silence"* (Ps. 115:17).

The pains of death surrounded me, and the pangs of Sheol [the world of the dead] *laid hold of me....Then I called upon the name of the LORD....I was brought low, and He saved me....For You have delivered my soul from death, my eyes from tears, and my feet from falling. I will walk before the LORD in the land of the living.*
(Ps. 116:3–4, 6, 8–9)

The prophet Jonah described his experience of facing death and the wonderful deliverance he received by the hand of the Lord:

The waters compassed me about....I went down to the bottoms of the mountains; the earth with her bars was about me for ever: yet hast thou brought up my life from corruption. (Jonah 2:5–6 KJV)

The patriarch Job was a righteous man of faith of whom the Lord boasted, *"There is none like him on the earth, a blameless and upright man"* (Job 1:8). Even Job faced the prospect of death with foreboding:

Leave me alone, that I may take a little comfort, before I go to the place from which I shall not return, to the land of darkness and the shadow of death, a land as dark as darkness itself, as the shadow of death, without any order, where even the light is like darkness. (Job 10:20–22)

According to the understanding of men in Old Testament days, the region of the departed dead was a tightly secured prison with bars and doors: *"Have the gates of death been revealed to you? Or have you seen the doors of the shadow of death?"* (Job 38:17). *"The earth with its bars closed behind me forever"* (Jonah 2:6).

It was into this shadowy region of death that Jesus our Lord descended, apparently swallowed up by the grave forever, suffering the same fate as men of faith had from all former generations. Death seemed to have triumphed—or had it?

JESUS DEFEATS DEATH

Job said, *"He…brings the shadow of death to light"* (Job 12:22). All Hades began to stir, as something incomprehensible began to happen within that realm of darkness and the shadow of death. Was it really true? Could it be? Yes! **Light** began to shine. The hearts of the entrapped men of faith quickened. They stirred to life again in the presence of the One in whom they had believed. The power of God came upon them. They became aware of an opening above them, as the glory of God began shining down on them from above.

Jesus, the Son of God, had torn open the bars and gates of Hades and had begun releasing the men and women of faith entombed there, some for millennia of time. The door was **open**! Myriads of believers from past ages began streaming upward into the light and glory of God. Hallelujah! The believers were forever changed; their faith was rewarded. A glorious realization filled their souls: We are free! What a triumph! What a deliverance!

Death had been swallowed up in victory (1 Cor. 15:54)! Time had been forever changed by eternity. The path of glory led upward, upward, as the parade of victory left the shadows of death far behind and entered into more and more glory, as the very gates of paradise itself, the realm of the heavenlies, swung wide open to receive them. What beauty! What liberty! What glory!

The resurrection and ascension of Jesus Christ had thus become far more than the release of Himself alone, but became the liberation of all mankind who believed. Men and women of faith from all human history entered their eternal home to be forever *"present with the Lord"* (2 Cor. 5:8) around the throne of God:

> *"When He ascended on high, He led captivity captive, And gave gifts to men." (Now this, "He ascended"; what does it mean but that He also first descended into the lower parts of the earth? He who descended is also the One who ascended far above all the heavens, that He might fill all things.)* (Eph. 4:8–10)

> *That through death He might destroy him who had the power of death, that is, the devil, and release those who through fear of death were all their lifetime subject to bondage.* (Heb. 2:14–15)

THE CHRISTIAN'S HOPE

From the time of the glorious resurrection and ascension of Christ into the heavenlies until now, the outlook of the Christian believer upon death has been wonderfully transformed from that of the Old Testament dispensation. The way into heaven and the throne of God is now open to all who believe. Instead of the foreboding prospect of entombment in the shadowy regions of Sheol or Hades, for the Christian believer there is now the wonderfully different expectation of moving upward into the glory of God at death, into the very presence of the Lord Himself. As Christ told the thief who believed in Him on the cross: *"Today you will be with Me in Paradise"* (Luke 23:43).

Experiencing God's Power in Worship

What a glorious New Testament difference we find in the affirmations of the apostle Paul about our destiny at death: *"For to me, to live is Christ, and to die is gain"* (Phil. 1:21)! Paul wrote further:

> *So we are always confident, knowing that while we are at home in the body we are absent from the Lord....We are confident, yes, well pleased rather to be absent from the body and to be present with the Lord.*   (2 Cor. 5:6, 8)

What a difference! What a revelation of glory to come! What a victory over death, hell, and the grave! What would have been an awful fate to the greatest men of faith under the Old Testament dispensation—stoning at the hands of an angry mob—now became for Stephen an occasion of a most glorious revelation:

> *When they heard these things they were cut to the heart, and they gnashed at him with their teeth. But he, being full of the Holy Spirit, gazed into heaven and saw the glory of God, and Jesus standing at the right hand of God....Then they cried out with a loud voice, stopped their ears, and ran at him with one accord; and they cast him out of the city....And they stoned Stephen as he was calling on God and saying, "Lord Jesus, receive my spirit."*
> (Acts 7:54–55, 57–59)

"Come up higher, Stephen! Rise from your earthly house and walk into the heavens, My son. Well done!" And Stephen marched into paradise itself through open doors. No wonder countless Christian martyrs went to their deaths with songs on their lips and heavenly visions in their hearts!

THE KINGDOM OF GOD IS HERE

Yet what does this heavenly vision mean to us now? Is it simply a destiny awaiting believers after death? Is it a comforting place to go for eternity? Or does the kingdom of heaven have an impact on our lives now? According to the New Testament, heaven is the realm of eternity that overlays everything in space and time right now, the unseen realm that is more real than what we see here on earth:

> *We do not look at the things which are seen, but at the things which are not seen. For the things which are seen are temporary, but the things which are not seen are eternal.* (2 Cor. 4:18)

Jesus reiterated the fact that the realm of heaven is an unseen realm, which operates powerfully here on earth. When the Pharisees asked Him when the kingdom of God would come in the future age, Jesus told them it was already here, operating in their midst, and they didn't even know it!

> *Now when He was asked by the Pharisees when the kingdom of God would come, He answered them and said, "The kingdom of God does not come with observation* [visual inspection]; *nor will they say, 'See here!' or 'See there!' For indeed, the kingdom of God is within* [among] *you."* (Luke 17:20–21)

> *But if I cast out demons with the finger of God, surely the kingdom of God has come upon you.* (Luke 11:20)

The New Testament begins its gospel message with the ringing declaration of John the Baptist, *"Repent, for the kingdom of heaven is at hand!"* (Matt. 3:2). If the kingdom of heaven operates here on earth, yet cannot be seen or observed by men, how can we know anything about it? Jesus gave a simple answer: *"Unless one is born again, he cannot see the kingdom of God"* (John 3:3). The new birth is a spiritual awakening; our eyes are opened by the Spirit of God to see and know things in the heavenly realm.

The heavenly realm is revealed to us by the Holy Spirit. That is how we are made aware of its existence:

> *Unless one is born of water and the Spirit, he cannot enter the kingdom of God....That which is born of the Spirit is spirit. Do not marvel that I said to you, "You must be born again."* (John 3:5–7)

> *"Eye has not seen, nor ear heard...the things which God has prepared for those who love Him." But God has revealed them to us through His Spirit....But the natural man does not receive the things of the Spirit of God, for they are foolishness to him; nor can he know them, because they are spiritually discerned.* (1 Cor. 2:9–10, 14)

It is by the Spirit of the Lord, therefore, that we are enabled to see the heavenly realm. This explains how the apostle John was able so marvelously to see and hear things in heaven and to declare them to us:

> *I was in the Spirit on the Lord's Day, and I heard behind me a loud voice, as of a trumpet, saying, "I am the Alpha and the Omega, the First and the Last," and, "What you see, write in a book and send it to the seven churches."* (Rev. 1:10–11)

> *After these things I looked, and behold, a door standing open in heaven. And the first voice which I heard was like a trumpet speaking with me, saying, "Come up here, and I will show you things which must take place after this." Immediately I was in the Spirit; and behold, a throne set in heaven, and One sat on the throne.* (Rev. 4:1–2)

HEAVENLY PLACES ON EARTH

Our understanding of heaven is limited because of the space-time framework of our human minds. We conceive of heaven as some physical place to which we can go, as in space travel, so that if we could go far enough, fast enough, and long enough, we would finally get there. As our knowledge of the vastness of space has grown, so much further and distant heaven has become. We imagine it as being at the end of space, beyond the last galaxy somewhere.

How absurd! If heaven cannot be seen by men here on earth, then if they searched the whole universe, they would never find it. The truth is that heaven exists as another dimension of reality altogether: an unseen realm of eternity, visible only through the revelation of the Spirit to those who have truly been born again. It is a heavenly realm that can radically transform things on earth.

As Christian believers, we have the exciting opportunity of participating in the knowledge of this heavenly realm. We are aware of things on earth with our natural senses and aware of the things in heaven by the revelation of the Holy Spirit.

Make no mistake about it, our awareness of heaven is not as clear as our understanding of things here on earth. We do not see things in heaven quite as clearly, and we still depend upon Scripture for the description of what heaven is like. But by the Holy Spirit, we can truly sense the powers of heaven, and we are aware of the moving of God's Spirit in the heavenly realm. At times of prophetic revelation, especially in high worship and in prayer, we can almost see the throne of God and know the fellowship of His presence in heaven. This is what is meant by the scriptural teaching that the believer may today be on earth and yet also be in heavenly places in Christ, seated on the church pew and at the same time seated with Christ:

> *According to the working of His mighty power which He worked in Christ when He raised Him from the dead and seated Him at His right hand in the heavenly places, far above all principality and power and might....And [He] raised us up together, and made us sit together in the heavenly places in Christ Jesus.* (Eph. 1:19–21; 2:6)

The mystery of Christ and His body, the church, encompasses both heaven and earth. Jesus is the God-man, the Incarnate Word, God in the flesh; and the church, which is His body, is at once upon earth and also in the heavenlies by the Spirit. Jacob saw it in a vision:

> *Then he dreamed, and behold, a ladder was set up on the earth, and its top reached to heaven; and there the angels of God were ascending and descending on it.* (Gen. 28:12)

Jehovah the Lord stood above the ladder and declared to Jacob His promise of the land of Canaan. When Jacob awakened from his dream, he exclaimed prophetically: *"How awesome is this place! This is none other than the house of God, and this is the gate of heaven!"* (Gen. 28:17).

The house of God, the church of Jesus Christ, is the gateway into heaven. Upon a ladder stretching from earth to heaven, magnificent angels of God were seen, ascending and descending in the glory of the Lord. Jacob could only cry out, *"How awesome is this place!"* And who is the ladder? Who is the meeting together of heaven and earth? It is our Lord Jesus Christ. Christ confirmed it to Nathanael: *"Hereafter you shall see heaven open, and the angels of God ascending and descending upon the Son of Man"* (John 1:51).

An open heaven! The realm of heaven above hovers over the Son of Man on the earth below as an unseen cloud of glory. John saw *"the Spirit descending from heaven like a dove"* (v. 32), and Mark recorded what the voice from heaven said: *"You are My beloved Son, in whom I am well pleased"* (Mark 1:11). Jesus is the link between heaven and earth; His fullness is now dwelling in *"the church, which is His body, the fullness of Him who fills all in all"* (Eph. 1:22–23).

THE TWO-WAY PASSAGE

Through Jesus, the church becomes the gateway into heaven and the ladder of ascent into the very presence of God, allowing believers to be united with Christ in the heavenlies while manifesting the glory of God here on earth as well. There were angels descending the ladder as well as those ascending, as the glory of God was brought down from heaven to be displayed on earth.

In the church, the body of Christ, *"the fullness of Him who fills all in all,"* there exists this wonderful and marvelous two-way passage. It allows us to ascend into the heavenly realm around the throne of God through the Holy Spirit and to be seated with Christ in heavenly places. At the same time, it allows the glory of God to descend from the heavenlies through His body into the earth. Through the church, there is a pathway to ascend into the glory of God, while at the same time, His glory descends to the earth. The church, like Christ Himself, is a paradox, a mystery; at the same time, it is both heavenly and earthly, divine and human.

Heaven has always existed in its splendor and glory around the throne of God, but its manifestation on earth until the time of Jesus Christ was remote, even separated from view by the firmament, the crystal sea, that barrier between heaven and earth. Certainly the Father never intended such a separation and distance between our lives on earth and our participation in the power and glory of the true worship of His presence in heaven. His eternal intention has always been to bring the heavenly life of worship into manifestation here on earth. The purpose of the coming of Jesus was to atone for sin by His death on the cross and to bring in the new birth so that men everywhere could again experience the kingdom of God and enjoy a restored relationship with the Father in a way that would once again unite God and men and heaven and earth.

If there has been this glorious reuniting of heaven and earth in the risen Christ and His church, why aren't we seeing in our Christian worship today more of a release of the power of praise and worship that characterizes the victorious atmosphere of heaven? Instead of the church demonstrating the union of the powers of heaven with life here on earth, that same barrier between heaven and earth that existed before Christ ever came seems to have grown over the centuries, especially in areas of church worship. Has the steady growth and accumulation of religious tradition over the centuries, be it Catholic, Orthodox, or Protestant, slowly choked out the glorious spontaneity and exuberance of worship that is truly born of God?

Is there not a greater glory and splendor in Christian worship that could be manifest today if we truly abandoned ourselves to the creativity of God's Spirit? Are we seriously considering what God Himself wants in our worship services? What is His desire for true worship? What would really please Him? How does God want to orchestrate our worship services to accomplish His purposes? God's will in the matter should definitely be sought by every pastor and church leader today. What is happening in heaven should be studied and appreciated, for we have been instructed to pray by our Lord: *"Your will be done on earth as it is in heaven"* (Matt. 6:10).

Experiencing God's Power in Worship

It is the contention of this book that one of the preeminent desires in God's heart is to display His glory on earth through the splendor and creativity of Christian worship, so that what is being gloriously done in the beauty of worship in heaven will also be expressed here on earth through the church.

Chapter 4

On Earth as It Is in Heaven

Jesus Christ came down from the Father to display His glory upon the earth. Consider these verses: *"This beginning of signs Jesus did in Cana of Galilee, and manifested His glory"* (John 2:11). *"And we beheld His glory, the glory as of the only begotten of the Father"* (John 1:14). *"This sickness is not unto death, but for the glory of God."* (John 11:4). *"I have glorified You on the earth. I have finished the work which You have given Me to do"* (John 17:4).

The display of the glory of God on the earth fulfilled the desire in the heart of God from the beginning. He cried out prophetically more than a millennium before Christ's incarnation, after the whole nation of Israel had defected from His call in the wilderness, vowing that in spite of their rebellion, there was coming a day when *"truly, as I live, all the earth shall be filled with the glory of the LORD"* (Num. 14:21).

THAT THE WORLD MAY KNOW

Since the desire in the Father's heart is to manifest His glory on earth, is it surprising to discover that of the two directions of passage on the divine ladder between heaven and earth, on which angels were seen ascending and descending in Jacob's vision, Jesus chose to emphasize the descending of the glory from heaven to earth? *"In this manner, therefore, pray...Your kingdom come [here]. Your will be done on earth as it is in heaven"* (Matt. 6:9–10).

This consuming desire in the heart of God to display His glory on earth should be uppermost in the prayer life of every Christian. For this reason, Jesus wanted to leave His disciples

39

on the earth, so that the world might come to know the Lord through their words and see His glory reflected in them.

> *I do not pray that You should take them out of the world, but...that the world may believe that You sent Me. And the glory which You gave Me I have given them...that the world may know that You have sent Me.*
>
> (John 17:15, 21–23)

HEAVEN ON EARTH

If Christ is not praying for the Father to take us out of the world, and if He has taught us to pray that His kingdom would come here, on earth, why are we praying and singing so enthusiastically about leaving this world and going to heaven? The modern wistfulness in American Christianity to "fly away to gloryland" may be missing the whole point of Scripture! God wants to make this earth the gloryland!

But what about Scriptures that seem to emphasize the other direction of our ascending to glory? In the same prayer in which Jesus said, *"I do not pray that You should take them out of the world"* (v. 15), He also prayed, just nine verses later, *"Father, I desire that they also whom You gave Me may be with Me where I am, that they may behold My glory"* (v. 24). Is being in the world and at the same time being where He is a contradiction? An error? Of course not! It is a paradox, contained in the very nature of the church itself.

Is it possible for us to be where He is and still be on earth? Can we be seated where He is in heavenly places, and yet, at the same time, also be on the earth to manifest His glory? Yes! It is through the Holy Spirit that we are *"made...alive together with Christ"* (Eph. 2:5), and by the power of the Spirit, God has *"raised us up together, and made us sit together in heavenly places in Christ Jesus"* (v. 6 KJV). This Scripture is in the present perfect tense; it does not say that He *will someday make* us sit together in heavenly places, but that He *has made* us sit together in heavenly places in Christ Jesus. This means now, while living our natural lives here on earth, we Christians, with the help of the Holy Spirit, can have insight and experience in the realm of the heavenlies. It is like living in two dimensions of existence at the same time—heaven and earth. Thus, the church ascends the divine ladder from the earth to the heavenlies by the power of the Holy Spirit. It is also through the agency of the Holy Spirit that the things of God and of Christ are brought down to earth to us from heaven. Thus, the glory of God can be said to descend to the church on earth.

> *However, when He, the Spirit of truth, has come, He will guide you into all truth....He will glorify Me, for He will take of what is Mine and declare it to you. All things that the Father has are Mine. Therefore I said that He will take of Mine and declare it to you.*   (John 16:13–15)

The church ascends into the glory of the heavenlies in Christ, and the Spirit of God descends from heaven to the church on earth. What a glorious paradox! His glory is revealed to us in the heavenlies, and His glory is revealed through us on earth. Such is the marvelous dual nature of the church; it is able to coexist in both the heavenly and earthly realms.

Jesus made statements to His disciples just before His death concerning how He would return to them and manifest Himself to them after His Resurrection and Ascension. These statements reveal truth about the heavenly and earthly nature of the church. Concerning the uniting of the church with Him in the heavenlies by the Holy Spirit, Jesus declared,

> *Let not your heart be troubled* [by the coming separation at Calvary]; *you believe in God, believe also in Me. In my Father's house are many mansions* [rooms or abiding places]; *if it were not so, I would have told you. I go to prepare a place for you. And if I go and prepare a place for you, I will come again and receive you to Myself; that where I am, there you may be also.*   (John 14:1–3)

Relating to the manifestation on earth of the glory of God in the church, just twenty verses later, Jesus also declared,

> *And I will pray the Father, and He will give you another Helper, that He may abide with you forever....I will not*

41

leave you orphans; I will come to you....If anyone loves Me,
he will keep my word; and My Father will love him, and
We will come to him and make Our home with him.

(vv. 16, 18, 23)

HEAVENLY PLACES

What a wonderful mystery the church of Jesus Christ is! He
receives us into abiding places in the heavenlies by the Spirit,
and yet the Father and the Son also make their home with us
here on earth! This is the glorious two-way movement of ascending and descending pictured on the divine ladder, which is
Christ and His body, that unites heaven and earth. In John
14:3, we are taken to be where Christ is; in verse 23, He comes
to be where we are! In John 17:24, we are to be with Him where
He is; in verse 15, we are to be left in the world to be clothed
with His glory! In John 14:2, we are to live in His house; in
verse 23, He makes His home in us. Thus the Christian can be
both *"in...heavenly places"* (Eph. 1:3) and on earth at the same
time.

I do not pray for these alone, but also for those who will be-
lieve in Me through their word; that they all may be one, as
You, Father, are in Me, and I in You; that they also may be
one in Us, that the world may believe that You sent Me.
And the glory which You gave Me I have given them, that
they may be one just as We are one: I in them, and You in
Me; that they may be made perfect in one, and that the
world may know that You have sent Me.   (John 17:20–23)

What a glorious, divine entanglement! Christ in us and we
in Him! He prays to the Father not to remove us from the earth,
but to display His glory though us to the world, so *"that the*
world may believe" (v. 21) and *"the world may know"* (v. 23).
Whatever is to be the ultimate destiny of the church in eternity,
whatever the final fulfillment of these passages will be, it must
be declared firmly that Jesus emphasized the manifestation of
the glory of God on earth through the church, not the removal
of the church from the earth.

The only way to properly conceive what the New Testament teaches about the nature of the church, which allows it to be both in the heavenlies and on earth simultaneously, is to understand that the realm of the heavenlies is not just another place on the natural plane of existence. It is neither separate nor far from the earth so that we are either *here* or *there*. The heavenly realm is another dimension of existence altogether that, in a sense, overlays or is associated with time and space (to use a popular twentieth-century concept—a kind of parallel universe).

Like the omnipresence of God, it is an unseen realm, more real, more permanent than anything in the physical world. We have been granted entrance into this heavenly realm and into the presence of the Lord Himself through the outpoured Spirit of God, so that we can be both *here* and *there* at the same time. We can be both here on earth and also in heavenly places in Christ. What a glorious mystery this is!

> *We do not look at the things which are seen, but at the things which are not seen. For the things which are seen are temporary, but the things which are not seen are eternal.* (2 Cor. 4:18)

Of course, treasures are laid up for us in heaven (Matt. 6:20), and there is a heavenly existence beyond our physical lives here on earth. All these things are still true, but the emphasis of Scripture is to direct our prayers and faith to the manifestation now, on earth, of the kingdom, power, and glory of God through the church of Jesus Christ: *"Your kingdom come. Your will be done on earth as it is in heaven"* (v. 10). And the ones who are truly able to manifest the glory of God on earth are those who also know the exaltation of the Spirit of God in heavenly places! *"He who descended is also the One who ascended far above all the heavens, that He might fill all things"* (Eph. 4:10).

> *That Christ may dwell in your hearts through faith; that you, being rooted and grounded in love, may be able to comprehend with all the saints what is the width and length and depth and height; to know the love of Christ*

> *which passes knowledge; that you may be filled with all the fullness of God.* (Eph. 3:17–19)

The desire in the heart of God is to cause His power and His glory to be visibly manifest in the Christian church here on earth. And in this momentous time, as we make the transition between millennia and face apocalyptic times, God is beginning to powerfully pour out His Spirit and to reveal His presence in a new wave of worship in the church of Jesus Christ. Those who *"hear what the Spirit* [is saying] *to the churches"* (Rev. 2:11) in this generation are hearing a new *"sound from heaven"* (Acts 2:2), as on the Day of Pentecost.

Chapter 5

Heaven on Earth

And I heard, as it were, the voice of a great multitude, as the sound of many waters and as the sound of mighty thunderings, saying, "Alleluia! For the Lord God Omnipotent reigns!"
—Revelation 19:6

His feet were like fine brass, as if refined in a furnace, and His voice as the sound of many waters.
—Revelation 1:15

The Christian church has been standing before the Lord of the whole earth repeating this prayer for centuries: *"Your will be done on earth as it is in heaven"* (Matt. 6:10). *"Your will be done on earth as it is in heaven." "Your will be done on earth as it is in heaven."*

What is the will of God being done in heaven that we have been praying for so diligently to happen here on earth? It is to worship the Father with complete adoration as the angels do who encircle the throne. We have been praying to the Father for centuries to pour out heavenly worship in the church on earth, and it is now beginning to happen. Yes, the worship of heaven, the thunderous praise, the waves of worship are pouring forth from hundreds of millions of voices. Countless worshipers surround the throne, crying out praises to the Lamb. What beauty! What glory! We are beginning to experience the rivers of praise, the *"sound of many waters,"* the cascading, reverberating noise of a multitude, a free-flowing tide of worship filled with the power of the Holy Spirit. It is really happening! The *"windows of heaven"* (Gen. 7:11) are being opened afresh in our day, and the waters of the Spirit *"above the firmament"* (Gen. 1:7) in the heavenly realm are now being poured out on the earth. Churches around the world are experiencing this heavenlike worship now.

OUR PRAISES ASCEND; HIS GLORY DESCENDS

A new revival of praise and worship is stirring in the church as the twentieth century draws to a close. In this present generation, the generation many feel will herald the return of the glory of Christ to the church in an unprecedented way, the worship of heaven is being poured out on the earth as churches worldwide are experiencing the presence of God in ways they have never known before. Worship services lasting an hour or more are not uncommon, as worship leaders, led by the Holy Spirit, are learning to blend *"psalms and hymns and spiritual songs"* (Eph. 5:19) into mighty rivers of praise and worship, lifting congregations into the very heights of heaven, into an experience of the spiritual atmosphere of worship around the very throne of God. Truly an ascending into the heights of God's presence and a descending of the glory of God on the church are occurring today.

Churches of all denominations are testifying to new, refreshing waves of worship in their midst as congregations are being released to praise and worship the Lord spontaneously in the Holy Spirit. The heavens are being opened during these times of worship, and divine prophetic insights manifested in gifts and ministries of the Holy Spirit are being displayed on a worldwide scale.

THE "SOUND OF MANY WATERS"

The characteristic mark of this revival of praise and worship in the church is the sound of spontaneous worship in the Holy Spirit. It is described as *"the sound of many waters"* or singing in the Spirit. Believers are learning to lift their voices to the Lord, pouring out their own words from their own hearts in a beautiful harmonious unity with Spirit-anointed musical instruments. *"Blessed are the people who know the joyful sound! They walk, O LORD, in the light of Your countenance"* (Ps. 89:15).

Glorious things are happening in this new kind of worship. Songs are being born right in the midst of praise services; subsequently, they have been shared around the world. Prophetic singing, reminiscent of the days of King David, is being restored. Spirits of worshipers are being set aflame by the power and glory of the Lord. It is a genuine restoration of the kind of worship and praise described in the Psalms.

Singing in the Spirit in times of spontaneous worship and praise is sweeping across the earth in our generation. As believers come together in services of worship and blend together the *"rivers of living water"* (John 7:38), which are resident within each of them by the Holy Spirit, a glorious, powerful, composite *"sound of many waters"* is being produced and is resounding in churches today.

The apostle John heard this *"sound of many waters"* thundering out of the churches of Asia in his own day and equated it with the voice of the Lord Himself:

> *Then I turned to see the voice that spoke with me. And having turned I saw seven golden lampstands* [the seven churches], *and in the midst of the seven lampstands One like the Son of Man...and His voice as the sound of many waters.* (Rev. 1:12–13, 15)

Throughout the Scripture, this *"sound of many waters"* is the characteristic voice of the Lord, sounding out from the redeemed church. It is heard in heaven as the song of the redeemed:

> *And I heard a voice from heaven, like the voice of many waters, and like the voice of loud thunder. And I heard the sound of harpists playing their harps. They sang as it were a new song before the throne.* (Rev. 14:2–3)

The *"sound of many waters"* is heard in heaven as the praise of the servants of the Lord:

> *Then a voice came from the throne, saying, "Praise our God, all you His servants."...And I heard, as it were, the voice of a great multitude, as the sound of many waters*

and as the sound of mighty thunderings, saying "Alleluia!
For the Lord God Omnipotent reigns!"   (Rev. 19:5–6)

John heard this sound of many waters, which was the expression of the voice of the Lord Himself in the midst of the seven lampstands. It was coming from the seven churches on earth (Rev. 1:20). His voice was *"as the sound of many waters"* (v. 15).

UNITED IN PRAISE

What produces this sound? It is the corporate manifestation of the Spirit of the Lord pouring forth from the saints in praise and worship before the throne of God. The myriads of saints who have been baptized with the Holy Spirit have become recipients of these *"rivers of living water"* (John 7:38), and these rivers flow out through uplifted voices, as words of praise, worship, thanksgiving, and prayer ascend to the very throne of God:

Jesus stood and cried, saying, "If anyone thirsts, let him come unto Me and drink. He who believes in Me, as the Scripture has said, out of his heart will flow rivers of living water. But this He spoke concerning the Spirit, whom those believing in Him would receive.   (John 7:37–39)

When the multitude of saints come together and raise their voices in public praise and worship, blending their rivers of the Holy Spirit, the corporate sound produced is the characteristic *"sound of many waters"* in the church, the totality of which becomes the voice of the Lord Himself singing through them. Speaking of Jesus praising the Father through the church, the author of Hebrews applied the glorious verse in Psalm 22:22 to Christ Himself, who is said to declare, *"In the midst of the assembly I will sing praise to You"* (Heb. 2:12).

In other words, Jesus sings His praise through the church, which is His body, by means of the rivers of the Holy Spirit poured out in worship to the Father. What a joy to be a part of that majestic voice of the Lord, sounding out from the churches in praise to God! What a privilege to stand in the congregation and participate in this grand and glorious *"sound of many waters"* around the throne!

"The sound of many waters" is not a distinct sound of one voice, but the undifferentiated sound of a multitude, a mass of people lifting their voices, all singing in the Spirit, blending harmoniously in a glorious river of praise. This unique, wonderfully individualized expression of praise allows each believer to pour out his own words from his own heart to His Lord, enabling him to express himself more freely in this fashion than with the words of any chorus or hymn ever written.

What a glory of God's greatness is revealed in such worship! He is able to gather to Himself the worship of countless millions of saints and yet receives each one individually in His presence, singled out from all the rest, as if no one else stood before Him. Each one becomes the one in millions who is able to commune with the Father in his own way and his own words, yet the millions are as one. United, they become the cascading sound of countless waterfalls, the noise of a multitude, the praise of a host, glorious in their beauty and harmony around the throne.

Ezekiel heard this unique sound associated with the glory of God, which was sent from heaven and moved on the earth through the *"living creatures"* (Ezek. 1:5) of his vision:

> *When they went, I heard the noise of their wings, like the noise of great waters, as the voice of the Almighty, the voice of speech* [a rushing sound, a windy roar], *as the noise of an host....This was the appearance of the likeness of the glory of the LORD.* (vv. 24, 28 KJV)

This sound is like the harmony created by the spontaneous singing in the Spirit that is being restored to the church today. No better description can be found of these times of worship when everyone lifts his voice and praises the Lord together, each in his own words, than the simple phrase, *"the sound of many waters."* It is an undifferentiated sound, like the noise of a multitude, yet a powerful sound, filled with all the force and energy of the Spirit of God.

THE SOUND AND THE GLORY

Ezekiel associated this sound with the glory of God that would be restored to the house of the Lord in the last days.

Experiencing God's Power in Worship

Behold, the glory of the God of Israel came from the way of the east. His voice was like the sound of many waters; and the earth shone with His glory....Behold, the glory of the LORD filled the temple. (Ezek. 43:2, 5)

The sound and the glory! The sound of the glory! The rivers of praise in the heavens around the throne of God that are now manifest in the earth through the church of Jesus Christ cascade in crescendos of praise and worship, no longer just in the courts of heaven, but also now in the house of God on earth.

Hear attentively the thunder of His voice, and the rumbling that comes from His mouth. He sends it forth under the whole heaven [on earth], His lightning to the ends of the earth. After it a voice roars; He thunders with His majestic voice....God thunders marvelously with His voice; He does great things which we cannot comprehend. For He says...'Fall on the earth'; likewise to the gentle rain and the heavy rain of His strength. (Job 37:2–6)

Do you know the ordinances of the heavens? Can you set their dominion over the earth? Can you lift up your voice to the clouds, that an abundance of water may cover you? (Job 38:33–34)

HEAVEN'S OPEN WINDOWS

In this apocalyptic generation, God is truly saying to the *"heavy rain of His strength," "Fall on the earth."* And in churches throughout the world, where the *"sound of many waters"* is heard, God's people are lifting their voices *"to the clouds,"* and the *"abundance of water"* from the heavens is covering them with the glory and presence of the Lord!

The windows of heaven are beginning to open, and divine thunderstorms of revival are being poured out on the church. This visitation of God bears a spiritual analogy to the days of Noah when *"the windows of heaven were opened"* (Gen. 7:11), *"the fountains of the great deep were broken up"* (v. 11), and a great rain from heaven poured out on the earth (v. 12).

God had originally created heaven and earth in a most unusual way, by making a firmament called heaven and then by placing waters both above the heaven and under the heaven:

Then God said, "Let there be a firmament in the midst of the waters, and let it divide the waters from the waters." Thus God made the firmament, and divided the waters which were under the firmament from the waters which were above the firmament; and it was so. And God called the firmament Heaven. (Gen. 1:6–8)

In the days of Noah, these *"windows of heaven"* were opened, and the waters that had stood above the heaven or firmament fell in upon the earth in a most awesome fashion, so much so that this magnificent rain washed the earth clean of wickedness and lifted the righteous in the ark of deliverance to a great salvation and a glorious new beginning.

REVIVAL RAINS

Not only did great rain fall from heaven, but great fountains of waters in the earth were released as well: *"On that day all the fountains of the great deep were broken up, and the windows of heaven were opened"* (Gen. 7:11).

Has God given us a spiritual picture of these last days in the natural events of the days of Noah? *"But as the days of Noah were, so also will the coming of the Son of Man be"* (Matt. 24:37). We are certainly seeing divine thunderstorms of revival rain beginning to fall on the earth today. The heavens are being opened, and the rivers of waters in the heavenlies are being poured out on the church of Jesus Christ. And the *"fountains of the great deep"* of the Holy Spirit within us are also pouring forth *"rivers of living water"* (John 7:38). Water pours down from heaven, and it also breaks out of the earth.

The noise of worship that has been hidden in the heavenly realm for millennia, the *"sound of many waters,"* is now being heard again in the church. We are experiencing a great deluge of God's rain on the earth, an outpouring of divine visitation and revival that is destined to sweep away all wickedness and lift the saints of God in the church, the ark, to enjoy full salvation and a glorious new beginning.

The Old Testament prophets cried out through the Holy Spirit concerning the great revival rains that would fall in the last days: *"Ask the LORD for rain in the time of the latter rain. The LORD will make flashing clouds; He will give them showers of rain"* (Zech. 10:1).

The prophet Hosea described the first and second comings of Christ in terms of the outpouring of rains of revival: *"He will come to us like the rain, like the latter and former rain to the earth"* (Hos. 6:3).

We know that Jesus poured out the *"former rain"* of Pentecost nearly two thousand years ago. Are we then to expect Him to come to us again in these last days with the outpouring of the *"latter rain"* of His presence as well? Many in the church of Jesus Christ in this generation are declaring emphatically, "Yes!"

What a glorious and magnificent outpouring of the Spirit of God occurred in the *"former rain"* of the Day of Pentecost! *"There came a sound from heaven"* (Acts 2:2), the sound of the glory of God. It was the *"sound of many waters."* The sound *"as of a rushing mighty wind...filled the whole house where they were sitting"* (v. 2).

God sent from heaven the atmosphere of praise and worship around His throne, borne on the wind of the Holy Spirit, that *"sound of many waters,"* that noise of a rushing, mighty wind, which surrounded all the disciples that glorious day. They were baptized into it, immersed in it, and overcome by it.

Intoxicated with the presence of God and the power of the Holy Spirit, they spilled out into Solomon's Porch, blending their own voices with the sound that came from heaven, pouring out their praises in all the languages of the nations to blend with the worship of the heavenlies. One hundred and twenty more voices were added to the millions on high.

> *There appeared to them divided tongues, as of fire, and one sat upon each of them. And they were all filled with the Holy Spirit and began to speak with other tongues, as the Spirit gave them utterance....And when this sound occurred, the multitude came together, and were confused, because everyone heard them speak in his own language...."We hear*

them speaking in our own tongues the wonderful works of God." (vv. 2:3–4, 6, 11)

THE DIVINE LADDER

The ladder that reached from earth to heaven and from heaven to earth was now complete. Christ, the ascended and exalted Lord, seated on His heavenly throne, was now united with His earthly body, the church, by means of the outpoured Holy Spirit, which at the same time lifted the disciples into the heavenly realm where Christ was and also brought the glory of God down to earth to be manifest where they were. They were where He was, and He was where they were. The marvelous two-way passage between heaven and earth was now functioning.

What a glory of God was manifest on the earth that Day of Pentecost! As the sound of the rushing, mighty wind of the Spirit blended with the upraised voices of the apostles and disciples, a great noise penetrated the surrounding regions of the city. It was the sound of heaven, the noise of many waters, the voice of the Almighty. It was the sound of our eternal home, the sound we were created to respond to, the sound of heaven that answers the cry in the hearts of men. It was a magnetic sound, drawing the multitudes together, a sound that no mere hundred and twenty people could ever produce on their own.

Thousands flocked together, drawn to the source of their ultimate release into the glory of God. They heard the sound of worship; they heard them magnifying God and telling His wonderful works in all the languages of earth. They saw the disciples moving with rejoicing and praise on their lips. Men of earth were responding to the presence of their Lord. As the disciples raised their voices in praise and adoration, the glory of God appeared among them: *"But You are holy, enthroned in the praises of Israel"* (Ps. 22:3). It was God Himself coming to dwell with His people. It was Christ the Lord, making His home with them. God had come to inhabit His body, the church.

ATTRACTED BY THE SPIRIT

The presence of the Lord is its own best advertisement, and the power of the Holy Spirit held a magnetic attraction to the people of that day: *"When this sound occurred, the multitude came together....Then they were all amazed and marveled"* (Acts 2:6–7).

From this multitude, drawn together by the supernatural sound from heaven, came over three thousand new believers. Three thousand! Then, quite possibly, over ten thousand had gathered! How hesitant we are in our Spirit-filled churches today to let the powerful sound of heavenly praise and worship go forth in our services. Will it offend? Will it alienate? Will it drive away? Of course not, for *"the multitude came together"* (v. 6).

Chapter 6

God in the Church

The powerful, spontaneous, creative Spirit of God infused life into the newly formed church. As the Spirit of God moved into the body of Christ on earth, marvelous things began to happen—not just on that special Day of Pentecost, when three thousand were swept into the kingdom of God and the city of Jerusalem was shaken to its foundations, but continuously thereafter, as the Spirit of God became active in the early church.

When the lame man at the temple gate was healed by the ministry of Peter and John, such a crowd gathered that five thousand believed in the Lord Jesus Christ (Acts 4:4). Hearing of the miraculous power of God, multitudes gathered from the surrounding cities to Jerusalem, and sick people were laid out in the streets in the hopes that just the shadow of Peter would fall upon them to heal them (Acts 5:15). People were raised from the dead. (See Acts 9:36–41.) Whole cities turned to the Lord. (See verses 32–35.) On at least three occasions, angelic visitations released the apostles from prison so that they could continue their preaching ministry. (See Acts 5:17–25; 12:3–11; 16:25–31.) The *"power from on high"* (Luke 24:49) was definitely at work, and the kingdom of God was operating explosively.

CREATIVE TOUCHES OF THE SPIRIT

One catches glimpses in the New Testament of the freshness and vitality in the worship services of the early church brought about by the creativity of the Spirit and presence of God. Each time a gathering of the church is recorded in the book of Acts, there is a unique emphasis, a special purpose brought forth by the Holy Spirit. A sense of awe and wonder must have excited the hearts of the early Christians as they realized that the God of heaven was actually in their midst to accomplish specific purposes.

Sometimes this divine creativity of the Holy Spirit produced an infusion of joy in the believers: *"And the disciples were filled with joy and with the Holy Spirit"* (Acts 13:52). At other times, the emphasis was on intense prayer as the church called on the Lord to work signs and wonders in the name of Jesus Christ: *"And when they had prayed, the place where they were assembled together was shaken; and they were all filled with the Holy Spirit, and they spoke the word of God with boldness"* (Acts 4:31).

On one occasion, teaching predominated, as the apostle Paul taught them the Word of God all night long. An interruption at midnight, which necessitated raising a young man from the dead, did not deter Paul from the emphasis on teaching that he sensed in the Holy Spirit. He continued speaking until dawn.

> *Paul...spoke to them and continued his message until midnight....And in a window sat a certain young man named Eutychus, who was sinking into a deep sleep....As Paul continued speaking, he fell down from the third story and was taken up dead. But Paul went down, fell on him, and embracing him said, "Do not trouble yourselves, for his life is in him." Now when he had come up, had broken bread and eaten, and talked a long while, even till daybreak, he departed.* (Acts 20:7, 9–11)

Whether it was the fullness of joy and the Holy Spirit or earthshaking prayer and intercession or intensive preaching and teaching of the Word, the early Christian gatherings were certainly characterized by the variety and creativity of the Spirit of God. What a refreshing contrast to the predictable, always-the-same church meetings in many places today. The same amount of time is allotted to the same functions in the same order with the same songs and same prayers (and sometimes even the same messages) week after month after year! Visualize the great God of Creation waiting in heaven for us to open our windows to the mighty creative breath of His Holy Spirit so that He can release life and variety into our services.

GOD IN US

The Lord God truly came to inhabit His church on earth in order to cause it to function as His body—the very vehicle of expressing the activity of His Spirit. The thought that God would manifest Himself on earth through men is staggering. King Solomon, not fully understanding the New Testament principle of God indwelling His people, looked at the temple he had just built, in spite of its earthly magnificence, and cried out, *"Will God indeed dwell with men on the earth?"* (2 Chron. 6:18). In answer to this question, the New Testament declares that God has indeed taken up residence by His Holy Spirit in the church of Jesus Christ and has filled it with His presence:

> *The church...is His body, the fullness of Him who fills all in all....That Christ may dwell in your hearts through faith; that you...may...know the love of Christ which passes knowledge; that you may be filled with all the fullness of God.* (Eph. 1:22–23; 3:17–19)

The New Testament church actually believed itself to be the body of Christ in action; they declared that Christ was acting through them corporately as He had done when He was on earth: healing through their hands, speaking through their mouths, and thinking through their minds. What a transforming realization! *"God was in Christ"* (2 Cor. 5:19)—the early church understood that. Now they also realized that Christ was in them (Col. 1:27) as well. Such an incarnation of God in His people had been prophesied by Zechariah hundreds of years earlier:

> *"Sing and rejoice, O daughter of Zion! For behold, I am coming and I will dwell in your midst," says the LORD. "Many nations shall be joined to the LORD in that day,*

*and they shall become My people. And I will dwell in your
midst."*   (Zech. 2:10–11)

Think of it: the Almighty God dwells in the midst of His
people—*"And the name of the city from that day shall be: THE
LORD IS THERE"* (Ezek. 48:35). Heaven has come down to earth!
We speak so casually of such truth, so glibly mentioning these
explosive New Testament teachings, claiming with a quick nod
of the head to know that "Jesus lives in my heart" or "The
presence of God is with me all the time." Yet do we actually realize what we are saying? The almighty God of heaven has, in
fact, come to dwell in us!

GOD AMONG US

We need only to turn to the Scriptures to find instances in
which the mighty, powerful presence of God actually did dwell
among His people to discover what an awesome experience it
really was. One such example was the glorious dedication cere-
mony of the temple of Solomon. One wonders if the singers and
musicians realized that day what was about to happen as they
took their positions in the temple area. All the preparations had
been so carefully made. One hundred and twenty trumpeters
were in their places, clothed in white linen. Other instruments—psalteries, harps, and cymbals—were arrayed around
the altar area, and the Levitical singers were standing in their
appointed positions, ready to worship and praise the Lord.

The magnificent ark of the covenant had been set in place
in the Holy of Holies, and all the elders, the heads of the tribes,
and the king himself had gathered for the glorious consecration
of the temple. When they began to worship, *"when the trumpeters and singers were as one, to make one sound to be heard in
praising and thanking the LORD"* (2 Chron. 5:13), then it happened: the magnificent glory of the Lord descended upon them:

*When they lifted up their voice with the trumpets and cym-
bals and instruments of music, and praised the LORD...the
house...was filled with a cloud, so that the priests could
not continue ministering because of the cloud; for the glory
of the LORD filled the house of God.*   (vv. 13–14)

We pass so lightly over descriptions such as these in Scripture. What a manifestation of the almighty presence of the Lord! A visible cloud actually filled the temple, a cloud so full of God's glory that it actually distilled into view. Yet even more important than the cloud that was seen was the invisible cloud, the all-encompassing presence of God Himself that was sensed so strongly by the priests of Israel that they could not even stand on their feet to minister.

As they continued in their service of worship before the Lord, Solomon mounted a platform in the sight of all the people and prayed a magnificent prayer, calling on the Lord to hear their petitions and to bless their land. When he had finished, the presence of God was powerfully displayed among them once again:

> *When Solomon had finished praying, fire came down from heaven and consumed the burnt offering and the sacrifices; and the glory of the LORD filled the temple. And the priests could not enter the house of the LORD, because the glory of the LORD had filled the Lord's house. When all the children of Israel saw how the fire came down, and the glory of the LORD on the temple, they bowed their faces to the ground on the pavement, and worshiped and praised the LORD.* (2 Chron. 7:1–3)

An unheard-of manifestation of God's glory had appeared to Israel that day. Greater than the appearance of the Lord to a single individual, such as Daniel, which caused him to fall on his face before the awesome majesty of the Lord's presence, the glory of God was so overwhelming on this great dedication day that a whole city fell prostrate on their faces before the Lord. They poured out their hearts in worship before Him. God, for a brief season, had come among them, filling their house of worship with His holy presence.

THE KEY OF DAVID

What had caused such an expression of God's glory to be shown in Israel that day? Is it possible for us to ever know such

59

splendor in our worship services in the present day, or are we to be content only to read about such things in Scripture? Amazingly, churches today are beginning to experience such wonderful manifestations of God's presence as they are rediscovering the *"key of David"* (Rev. 3:7), which opened the door that day in the temple of Solomon to such outpourings of the glory of God: *"These things says He who is holy, He who is true, He who has the key of David, He who opens and no one shuts"* (v. 7).

What is this *"key of David"* that manifests the glorious presence of the almighty God in our worship services today? The answer is profoundly simple: the faithful practice of praise and worship, involving singers and musicians, anointed, appointed, and dedicated to this ministry, utilizing all the forms of worship found in the Psalms. King David made praise and worship the cornerstone of his tabernacle services in Zion. He appointed rotating courses or shifts of singers and instrumentalists who praised the Lord day and night, so that a continuous incense of praise and worship was always ascending to the Lord. (See 1 Chronicles 25:7–31.)

David's priesthood worshiped the Lord in abandonment and true liberty in the Holy Spirit, expressing their worship with the lifting of hands; with clapping and rejoicing; with dancing, bowing, and prostrating themselves before the Lord; and with prophesying new songs in the Holy Spirit. King David learned by experience that when his praising priesthood began to worship the Lord in faith, the prophetic presence of God was manifest among them in liberty and glory.

And David passed on this key to his son, Solomon, not only giving him instructions about how to build the temple, but also how to prepare the priesthood to worship the Lord on that great dedication day. When everything was set in order before the Lord and all the priests had been sanctified (cleansed); when the trumpeters were in their places; when the players on psalteries, harps, and cymbals were ready; when the singers were prepared for worship; and when the leaders of the nation were present before the Lord; then the *"key of David"* operated powerfully as the divine glory of God came down on them at the precise moment when the praises began:

> *It came to pass, when the trumpeters and singers were as one, to make one sound to be heard in praising and thanking the LORD, and when they lifted up their voice with the trumpets and cymbals and instruments of music, and praised the LORD...that the house...was filled with a cloud...for the glory of the LORD filled the house of God.*
>
> (2 Chron. 5:13–14)

David and Solomon had discovered a simple but profound truth: when worshipers praise the Lord, the divine presence of God is manifest among them. Why? Because Davidic praise and worship is the recreation on earth of the same atmosphere of worship that exists in heaven around the throne of God.

It is a manifestation in time and space of the worship of eternity. It brings into being here on earth what is happening in the heavenly realm, and it draws the attention of the Almighty. If the Father is seeking those who will worship Him *"in spirit and truth"* (John 4:23), when He actually does find them, He will come down to them with divine confirmations of His presence and dwell among them, for His Spirit has found a resting place there. This was the secret of David's tabernacle worship on Mount Zion, a secret expressed in a simple but profound way: *"But thou art holy, O thou that inhabitest the praises of Israel"* (Ps. 22:3 KJV).

GOD'S RESPONSE

When David erected his new tabernacle on Mount Zion and appointed singers and musicians to worship and praise the Lord there continuously, God loved it. He could not restrain Himself. He had to go down and be in them: *"For the LORD has chosen Zion; He has desired it for His dwelling place. 'This is My resting place forever; here I will dwell, for I have desired it'"* (Ps. 132:13–14).

Why such an exclamation of joy from the Father's heart when Zion was born? Why such love poured out from God on the worshipers there? Because for the first time in history, ritualistic, ceremonial approaches to God were discarded, and men entered directly into a personal relationship with Him through beautifully inspired praise and worship. The new order of the priesthood in Zion did nothing else but worship the Lord with singing accompanied by musical praise on their instruments. God loved it. It was so refreshingly different from the traditional ceremonies of the other "church" in David's day, the tabernacle of Moses, where in silence the priests routinely lit candles, burned incense, set forth bread every Sabbath, cleansed themselves in the holy water of purification, and offered animal sacrifices.

Even though God had originally ordained every detail of these ceremonial acts of Moses' tabernacle hundreds of years earlier, as soon as King David's worship services began, God transferred His presence from the tabernacle of Moses and placed His glory instead upon the tabernacle of David with its joyful praise, its prophetic songs of the Spirit, and its free expressions of worship. Asaph, the chief musician of David's tabernacle in Zion, sang about this transfer of God's glory from Moses' tabernacle to David's:

He forsook the tabernacle of Shiloh, the tent He had placed among men [Moses' tabernacle]....*But chose the tribe of Judah, Mount Zion which He loved* [site of David's tabernacle].   (Ps. 78:60, 68)

God dramatically illustrated this transfer of His presence from Moses' tabernacle to David's by the path of the ark of the covenant itself. When Israel took the ark out of the Holy of Holies in Moses' tabernacle and brought it into battle against the Philistines during the days of Eli the priest, God allowed it to be captured by the enemy because of the sin and corruption of Eli's sons. (See 1 Samuel 4.) This meant that from that time on, the priests in Moses' tabernacle were performing their religious ceremonies of candles, incense, bread, purification water, and animal sacrifice, and nothing was in the Holy of Holies to spiritually back up what they were doing. Instead of the radiance of the glory of God glowing upon the mercy seat on the ark, there was now only a black hole behind the veil. The name of Eli's grandson, born at that time, described what had happened: *"Ichabod"*—*"the glory has departed"* (1 Sam. 4:21–22). God had gone:

So that He forsook the tabernacle of Shiloh [that Moses built], *the tent He had placed among men....Moreover He rejected the tent of Joseph, and did not choose the tribe of Ephraim* [where Shiloh was].   (Ps. 78:60, 67)

A New Way of Worship

Later, after the ark had been returned to Israel, King David did not put it back in the tabernacle of Moses where it used to be, but he did something radically new. He put the ark in a new tabernacle, which he built on Mount Zion, the City of David, part of Jerusalem. (See 1 Chronicles 15:1; 2 Samuel 5:7.) He then ordained a new priesthood of worshipers to praise the Lord there *"continually before the ark of the covenant of God"* (1 Chron. 16:6 KJV).

What an unheard of boldness! Where did David get the authority to do such a thing? Didn't he realize that no one was ever permitted in the same room with the ark except the high priest once a year on the Day of Atonement? Didn't he know that the glory of God that rested on the ark had always re-mained hidden behind the veil in the Holy of Holies? And now, without a single scriptural command to do so, David was ap-pointing singers and musicians to worship the Lord *"continually before the ark of the covenant of God"* in his new tabernacle.

Instead of rebuking him for this radical decision, God did just the opposite. He took His glory off Moses' tabernacle and placed it squarely on David's, indicating by prophecy His divine approval of the worship services in Zion. As the worshipers in David's tabernacle sang, shouted, and praised the Lord on all manner of instruments, God Himself was in their midst, prophesying and singing through them. No wonder God told Samuel concerning David, *"The Lord has sought for Himself a man after His own heart"* (1 Sam. 13:14).

The Lord didn't even have to send a prophet to tell him what to do, and David didn't have to spend forty days of fasting on the mountaintop like Moses to find out what the will of God was. David did it automatically out of his own heart. *"I have found David the son of Jesse, a man after My own heart, who will do all My will"* (Acts 13:22).

Experiencing God's Power in Worship

God had allowed David to follow the desire of his heart and bring a priesthood and a nation into a relationship with Him through worship and praise. By doing so, He revealed a principle of heaven that was being manifest in Zion, namely this: that true worship brings us into the very presence of God. Such a profound principle is simply stated: God has allowed us to *"come before His presence with singing....Enter into His gates with thanksgiving, and into His courts with praise"* (Ps. 100:2, 4).

THE ZION PRINCIPLE

What a simple key! What a profound revelation! The dynamic secret of heaven has now become the secret of the spiritual success of Mount Zion. God lives in the heavenly atmosphere of worship, and in Zion, His will was now being done *"on earth as it is in heaven"* (Matt. 6:10). The presence of God was now manifest in the worship atmosphere of David's tabernacle, which had now become heaven on earth.

How God loved Zion! Mention of His love for it occurs often in the prophetic psalms:

> *The LORD loves the gates of Zion more than all the dwellings of Jacob. Glorious things are spoken of you, O city of God!...Both the singers and the players on instruments say, "All my springs are in you."* (Ps. 87:2–3, 7)

> *For the LORD has chosen Zion; He has desired it for His dwelling place: "This is My resting place forever; here I will dwell, for I have desired it....Her saints shall shout aloud for joy."* (Ps. 132:13–14, 16)

Because of David's deep love for God, God allowed him to move a whole priesthood into a New Testament understanding of the sacrifice of praise a thousand years before Calvary. God loves the Zion principle of worship and praise in any age. The same secret that brought the prophetic presence of God to the worship services in David's tabernacle on Mount Zion three thousand years ago is also working now as we begin a new millennium. Churches everywhere are returning to the simple worship and praise expressions found in the Psalms and are experiencing the same manifestations of the prophetic presence of God now, as then.

We are learning that Davidic worship brings an eternal response from God; as we praise Him, He manifests Himself in our worship services. The manifestation of God's glory in Zion in David's day was only an expression on earth of the eternal Zion principle: that God dwells forever in the praises of His people, in heaven or on earth, in time or in eternity. Whenever God is worshiped in Spirit and in truth, there Zion is, for there the will of God is being done *"on earth as it is in heaven"* (Matt. 6:10). Jesus Himself taught us the universal nature of true worship, that it is no longer localized on a single *"Holy Mountain"* (Zech. 8:3), but it is now spread throughout the whole earth:

> *The woman said to Him...."Our fathers worshiped on this mountain, and you Jews say that in Jerusalem is the place where one ought to worship." Jesus said to her, "Woman, believe me, the hour is coming when you will neither on this mountain, nor in Jerusalem, worship the Father....The hour is coming, and now is, when the true worshipers will worship the Father in spirit and truth."*
> (John 4:19–21, 23)

The worship principle that began in earthly Zion in the days of David has now been extended throughout the whole earth by the church of Jesus Christ, wherever men *"worship the Father in spirit and truth"* according to the Scripture. This is why the author of Hebrews could declare concerning the church universal:

> *But you have come to Mount Zion and to the city of the living God, the heavenly Jerusalem...to the general assembly and church of the firstborn who are registered in heaven...to Jesus the Mediator of the new covenant.*
> (Heb. 12:22–24)

LET PRAISE BEGIN

The church is forever linked to Zion. It is an expression of the eternal worship principle that pervades the heavens. It is therefore no surprise to find worship expressions of the Psalms and prophetic manifestations of the Spirit of God occurring everywhere in Christian churches today. If the church has truly *"come to Mount Zion,"* then let us begin to worship God accordingly.

We need to teach our churches today how to order their worship services as the worshipers did in the days of the Psalms. We need to create the expectancy of faith in our congregations by teaching them from the Psalms and from the history of King David how the Spirit of God moved on the worshipers in ancient times. We need to inspire our Spirit-filled churches to believe that God can move in our services today with the same prophetic ministry as in the days of old, as new songs of the Spirit are brought forth in our worship.

We need to make praise and worship a definite priority in our church services, giving a significant amount of time to it, pursuing this ancient and eternal ministry to the Lord with both diligence and enthusiasm. We need to prayerfully appoint singers and musicians in our churches who will faithfully worship the Lord with their voices and instruments. And we need to set our congregations free to experience the glorious liberty of all the forms of worship expression found in the Psalms. Churches that are doing these things are experiencing an unprecedented manifestation of the glory and presence of the Lord as in the days of David and Solomon and of the early church itself.

Chapter 7

Davidic Worship: Old or New Testament?

What a kinship Christian churches have with King David and his worship! It is almost as if three thousand years of intervening history never really existed. Prophetic new songs are being sung today with the same emphases as in the days of the Psalms, as churches everywhere are declaring the majestic glory and beauty of the Lord, God's triumphant victory over all His enemies, and the glorious worldwide reign of His kingdom.

Worship expressions are spontaneously emerging now in Christian worship services. Churches have discovered worship with uplifted hands and clapping, dances of joy and spontaneous prophetic praise, and then have learned with joy that these worship expressions are being experienced on a worldwide scale. Churches have even been sovereignly led by the Holy Spirit into forms of worship that they have later found confirmed in Scripture, such as worship dances in circles and lines, reminiscent of the Jewish culture. They have discovered that all these forms of worship movement are described in the various Hebrew words in the Old Testament simply translated *dance* in English.

KING DAVID'S NEW TESTAMENT WORSHIP MODEL

This rediscovery of the worship forms of the Psalms has led to such an intense interest in and study of Davidic praise that some have wondered if this restoration of Davidic worship forms might signal a return to outmoded Old Testament law. Nothing could be further from the truth! When we study the Psalms, we find to our amazement that King David received a New Testament understanding of praise and worship a thousand years early. He was actually a millennium ahead of his time.

Instead of being locked into the religious history of Israel, David and his singers prophesied that animal sacrifice was ultimately meaningless to God and exhorted men to offer to the Lord, instead of animals, the true sacrifices of praise and thanksgiving, a doctrine later confirmed in the New Testament: *"I will praise the name of God with a song, and will magnify Him with thanksgiving. This also shall please the LORD better than an ox or bull, which has horns and hooves"* (Ps. 69:30–31).

God prophesied in song through Asaph, the chief musician in David's tabernacle, rebuking the people with a divine sarcasm for believing that God actually wanted animals offered to Him:

> *I will not take a bull from your house, nor goats out of your folds. For every beast of the forest is Mine, and the cattle on a thousand hills....If I were hungry, I would not tell you; for the world is Mine, and all its fullness. Will I eat the flesh of bulls, or drink the blood of goats? Offer to God thanksgiving, and pay your vows to the Most High.*
> (Ps. 50:9–10, 12–14)

We find in the Psalms an amazing confirmation of the New Testament teaching that we are to *"continually offer the sacrifice of praise to God, that is, the fruit of our lips, giving thanks to His name"* (Heb. 13:15). King David sang it this way:

> *O Lord, open my lips, and my mouth shall show forth your praise. For You do not desire sacrifice [of animals], or else I would give it; You do not delight in burnt offering. The sacrifices of God are a broken spirit, a broken and a contrite heart; these, O God, You will not despise.*
> (Ps. 51:15–17)

A MATTER OF THE HEART

David realized that mere outward conformity to external rituals, such as the sacrifice of animals, was not what God wanted at all, even though He had originally ordained it. David understood that true worship was a matter of the heart and that what pleased the Lord was the joyful praise of our lips, poured forth from hearts full of thanksgiving and love. He knew that true worship is a matter of communication with the Lord, not merely conforming to religious rituals.

Several centuries after David, the prophet Jeremiah declared what later became a central doctrine of the New Testament Gospel—that God would take His laws of righteousness, and instead of inscribing them on external tablets of stone, as in the Old Testament, He would write them internally, within the hearts of His people (Jer. 31:31, 33). The book of Hebrews applies this prophecy of Jeremiah directly to the New Testament:

> *Behold, the days are coming, says the LORD, when I will make a new covenant* [or testament] *with the house of Israel and with the house of Judah....For this is the covenant that I will make with the house of Israel:...I will put My laws in their mind and write them on their hearts; and I will be their God, and they shall be My people*
>
> (Heb. 8:8, 10)

Hundreds of years before the time of Jeremiah and a millennium before the New Testament church, King David had already received this same revelation by the Holy Spirit—that God wanted heart righteousness, not animal sacrifice.

> [Animal] *sacrifice and* [burnt] *offering You did not desire....Burnt offering and sin offering You did not require....I delight to do Your will, O my God, and Your law is within my heart. I have proclaimed the good news of righteousness in the great assembly.* (Ps. 40:6, 8–9)

THE GIFT OF RIGHTEOUSNESS

Even though the righteousness of Christ had not yet been provided on Calvary, David knew by faith that God would one day clothe us with righteousness so that we could enter in *"behind the veil"* (Heb. 6:19) into His presence forever. David prayed concerning Zion: *"Let Your priests be clothed with right-eousness, and let Your saints shout for joy"* (Ps. 132:9). God an-swered this prayer by prophetically declaring in the same psalm: *"I will also clothe her priests with salvation, and her saints shall shout aloud for joy"* (v. 16).

We know that this prophecy was fulfilled in the New Tes-tament and established for us on Calvary. We know that we have been clothed with the righteousness of Christ forever. What is amazing is that David and his worshipers in Zion re-ceived this same understanding a thousand years before it was revealed in the New Testament!

King David and the New Testament church, therefore, had a common ground in both theology and practice. Davidic wor-ship is definitely New Testament. Theologically, David under-stood that our righteousness comes not by *"works of the law"* (Gal. 2:16), but by being *"clothed"* (Ps. 132:9) by the righteous-ness of God as a gift of grace. David also understood that God does not desire the sacrifice of animals, but the New Testament *"sacrifice of praise"* (Heb. 13:15).

In addition, David's worshipers also experienced a New Tes-tament prophetic anointing and the gifts of the Holy Spirit. Their services were charismatic in the truest sense of the word, for they were *"filled with the Spirit, speaking to one another in psalms and hymns and spiritual songs"* (Eph. 5:18–19). Their worship services were saturated with the ministry of prophecy.

DAVID'S PROPHETIC MINISTRY

This gift of prophecy, which the apostle Paul taught that we should *"covet"* above all others (see 1 Corinthians 12:31; 14:1), characterized the services of the New Testament church:

> *But if all prophesy, and an unbeliever or an uninformed person comes in, he is convinced by all....For you can all prophesy one by one, that all may learn and all may be en-couraged.* (1 Cor. 14:24, 31)

The ministry of prophecy became a hallmark of the worship of David's tabernacle. His psalms are the most prophetic portion of the Old Testament, quoted more often in the New Testament than any other book. No wonder the early Christians realized that the church was an expression of Zion, for all that happened in New Testament worship was linked not with the Old Testament Levitical system of animal sacrifice and the tabernacle of Moses, but instead was a manifestation of the Davidic sacrifice of praise and an experience of the prophetic presence of God.

RITUAL OR REALITY

David knew the true reality of God's presence; Moses' rituals only represented it symbolically. Moses instituted the symbol; David experienced the reality. Moses' priests burned physical incense on the altar; David's services were filled with the spiritual incense of praise, worship, and prayer. Moses' priests burned candles, with wicks saturated in olive oil; David's worshipers were themselves the wicks, saturated with prophetic oil and set aflame by the fire of the Holy Spirit. Moses' law commanded bread to be set forth in the tabernacle every Sabbath; David's worshipers sang and prophesied the spiritual Bread of Heaven, the Word of God.

It is true that David's priests had not yet experienced the regeneration and new birth of the New Testament Gospel and so could not enjoy the continuous abiding presence of the indwelling Christ, but the priesthood in Zion knew the same manifestations of the prophetic Holy Spirit that occurred in the New Testament church. It is remarkable that the Davidic priesthood moved in such great power and manifestation of God's prophetic presence without ever having experienced the new birth and the baptism of the Holy Spirit.

It is true that the animal sacrifices that Moses instituted were continued during the days of David and Solomon (see 1 Chronicles 16:1; 2 Chronicles 5:6), because Christ, the Lamb of God, had not yet been sacrificed. Yet David and the worshiping priesthood in his tabernacle in Zion moved far beyond the Old Testament Levitical system of animal sacrifice into a full New Testament expression of worship and praise, which was filled with God's prophetic presence.

71

Experiencing God's Power in Worship

It is this kinship between David and the New Testament church that caused the author of Hebrews to declare that we in the Christian church have not come to Mount Sinai, the origin of the Old Covenant, but we have *"come to Mount Zion"* (Heb. 12:22), the place of Davidic worship and praise.

Peter confirmed this fact, stating that Jesus Christ is the chief cornerstone laid in Zion, the church, and that in this New Testament house of God *"spiritual sacrifices,"* not animals, are to be offered:

> *You also, as living stones, are being built up a spiritual house* [the church], *a holy priesthood, to offer up spiritual sacrifices acceptable to God through Jesus Christ. Therefore it is also contained in the Scripture, "Behold I lay in Zion* [the church] *a chief cornerstone, elect, precious, and he who believes on Him will by no means be put to shame."*
>
> (1 Pet. 2:5–6)

In light of this overwhelming evidence that the New Testament church and the tabernacle of David are part of the same revelation of Zion, how can anyone believe that a restoration of Davidic worship is a return to Old Testament law? King David possessed a New Testament missionary spirit. He was the one to whom the Holy Spirit revealed that all nations, (Gentiles), would one day be praising the Lord. Worshipers in the tabernacle of David declared this fact in prophetic song:

> *Praise the LORD, all you Gentiles! Laud Him, all you peoples!* (Ps. 117:1).

> *All nations* [Gentiles] *whom You have made shall come and worship before You, O Lord, and shall glorify Your name.* (Ps. 86:9)

> *All the ends of the world shall remember and turn to the LORD, and all the families of the nations* [Gentiles] *shall worship before You.* (Ps. 22:27)

> *Yes, all kings shall fall down before Him; all nations shall serve Him....His name shall endure forever....And men*

72

shall be blessed in Him; all nations [Gentiles] *shall call Him blessed.* (Ps. 72:11, 17)

King David was not locked into the same self-righteous, legalistic, religious pride as were the Pharisees of Jesus' day. He was of a different spirit, for he possessed a worldwide missionary vision. He and his son, Solomon, knew by experience the evangelistic impact of praise and worship on the Gentiles. In the days of Solomon, which marked the high point of the glorious worship that had begun with David, all the nations of the earth were attracted to the glory of God revealed through the temple worship of Israel. Kings sent gifts and tribute money, and ambassadors from surrounding nations traveled to Jerusalem to behold the magnificence of the Lord:

So King Solomon surpassed all the kings of the earth in riches and wisdom. Now all the earth sought the presence of Solomon to hear his wisdom, which God had put in his heart. Each man brought his present: articles of silver and gold, garments, armor, spices, horses, and mules, at a set rate year by year. (1 Kings 10:23–25)

When the queen of Sheba arrived in Jerusalem and saw the blessings of God on Israel, especially when she saw Solomon's worship, *"his entryway by which he went up to the house of the LORD"* (v. 5), all her pride melted away. *"There was no more spirit in her"* (v. 5), and she broke out in worship: *"Blessed be the LORD your God, who delighted in you....Because the LORD has loved Israel forever"* (v. 9).

It was the presence of the Lord manifest in praise and worship that touched her heart so deeply and opened her spirit to God. God's glory was manifest in Israel in those days, through worshiping choirs and orchestras: *"Four thousand praised the LORD with musical instruments, 'which I made,' said David, 'for giving praise'"* (1 Chron. 23:5).

King David must have learned from experience that when prophetic gifts were manifested in the worship services of his tabernacle, these new songs of the Spirit had a strong evangelistic impact upon people. This kind of prophetic ministry must have been displayed in the presence of unbelievers in order for David to see the power of God's presence influencing them, for he sang: *"He has put a new song in my mouth; praise to our God; many will see it and fear, and will trust in the LORD"* (Ps. 40:3).

King David might have made a better missionary than even the New Testament apostles, for his heart was already opened to the nations because of the prophetic vision of universal worship he had received from the Lord in the new songs of Zion. The New Testament apostles needed miraculous signs and wonders and countless proofs of God's confirming hand, as well as several church councils full of heated debates, in order to finally accept the fact that it was really God's will not only to bless the Gentiles, but also to bring them into the church. King David would have had no problem with Gentiles getting blessed by God. He was the one who prophesied it would happen.

Interestingly, it was the tabernacle of David to which the early apostles appealed to establish the truth that God did in fact desire to save the Gentiles. During the great argument in the church council in Jerusalem concerning whether Gentiles who had believed in Christ should be allowed into the church without first becoming Jews by becoming circumcised and keeping the law, the apostle James settled the issue. He quoted the prophecy of Amos that when the tabernacle of David was restored in the last days, it would bring about the salvation of the Gentiles:

> *James answered, saying, "Men and brethren, listen to me: Simon [Peter] has declared how God at the first visited the Gentiles to take out of them a people for His name. And with this the words of the prophets agree, just as it is written: 'After this I will return and will rebuild the tabernacle of David, which has fallen down; I will rebuild its ruins, and I will set it up; so that the rest of mankind may seek the LORD, even all the Gentiles who are called by My name, says the LORD.'"* (Acts 15:13–17)

James' argument was simple and direct: When the tabernacle of David is restored in the last days, Gentiles will be saved.

Davidic Worship: Old or New Testament?

Gentiles are now being saved. Therefore the church is experiencing the fulfillment of the prophecy of the restoration of the tabernacle of David.

The prophecy of Amos is even more specific, declaring that the very purpose of the restoration of the tabernacle of David in the last days was to be evangelistic—to gather in the heathen: *"On that day I will raise up the tabernacle of David...that* [it] *may possess...all the Gentiles"* (Amos 9:11–12).

The restoration of Davidic worship in the church today is as much a direct fulfillment of prophecy as it was in the New Testament church. All the manifestations of spiritual gifts in the church in this generation, all the liberty and rejoicing in worship, and all the forms of praise in the Psalms being restored today represent a direct fulfillment of the prophecy of Amos that in these last days, God would *"raise up the tabernacle of David, which has fallen down, and...rebuild it as in the days of old"* (v. 11). The church of Jesus Christ is experiencing today this restoration of Davidic worship. Davidic worship is therefore very much New Testament.

THE CAUSE AND EFFECT

Jesus Himself made this relationship clear when He said, *"I am the Root and the Offspring of David"* (Rev. 22:16). Oh, the glorious mystery of the incarnation! Can we fully appreciate the significance of Jesus being the *"Root...of David"*? Jesus was the *"Root,"* or source, of everything that grew in David's ministry. He was the source of David's worship and praise, the origin of his prophetic gifts, the foundation of his kingdom, and the reason for his mighty victories in battle. Peter authoritatively preached on the Day of Pentecost that Jesus was also David's offspring, who had been raised up by God to sit on David's throne and to reign forever as King of Kings and Lord of Lords. (See Acts 2:29–36.)

What a marvelous evidence of the eternity of Christ! He is both the cause and the effect of David's worship, *"the Root and the Offspring of David"* (Rev. 22:16), *"the Alpha and the Omega, the beginning and the end"* (Rev. 1:8). He is the Son who has the name, and therefore the nature of, *"Everlasting Father"* (Isa. 9:6). *"For unto us a Child is born, unto us a Son is given....And His name will be called...Everlasting Father"* (v. 6).

"Hosanna to the Son of David!" (Matt. 21:9), they cried in Jerusalem that day, as Jesus entered in triumphal procession. The kingdom that began with David is now being extended throughout all the world by the church of Jesus Christ. Today, the church can enter with confidence into the joyful liberty and power of the worship of the Psalms and can experience the same prophetic manifestations as occurred in the days of David. Both the tabernacle of David and the New Testament church are expressions of the same spiritual Zion, which is heavenly worship on the earth:

> *But you have come to Mount Zion and to the city of the living God, the heavenly Jerusalem, to an innumerable company of angels, to the general assembly and church of the firstborn who are registered in heaven, to God the Judge of all, to the spirits of just men made perfect, and to Jesus the Mediator of the new covenant.* (Heb. 12:22–24)

The earthly expression of Mount Zion in Spirit-filled worship and praise is to become so universal that it will not only unite all kindred, tribes, and tongues in one last great harvest, but it will also include the ancient people of Israel as well.

The apostle Paul expressed this prophetic vision for the future very clearly. He testified to an intense desire in his heart *"for Israel...that they may be saved"* (Rom. 10:1). He viewed his apostolic commission to build up the Gentile church as having a longer range objective of "provoking" Jews to jealousy, so that they would desire to receive the grace of Christ as well. (See Romans 11:11–14.) He saw the church of Jesus Christ in the last days showing mercy to the Jews, so that by faith, they may be drawn into the universal Body of Christ. (See Romans 11:28–31.)

What a glorious vision for the culmination of church history! The apostle Paul taught that the inclusion of the believing Jews in the last days would bring forth resurrection life:

Davidic Worship: Old or New Testament?

For if their being cast away is the reconciling of the world, what will their acceptance be but life from the dead?
(Rom. 11:15)

Paul taught that God in His wisdom planned to rescue both Jew and Gentile out of disobedience and doubt. In the days of the early church, it was the Gentiles who were the unbelievers upon whom God had mercy. In the last days of the church, it will be the unbelieving Jews whom God will save by His mercy:

For as you were once disobedient to God, yet have now obtained mercy through their disobedience, even so these also have now been disobedient, that through the mercy shown you they also may obtain mercy. For God has committed them all to disobedience, that He might have mercy on all.
(Rom. 11:30–32)

In view of this prophetic vision, is God preparing the present-day church to be more attractive to the Jews? As they turn to Christ and are added to the church, will they find in Davidic worship and praise the full liberty and expression of the Psalms and the spiritual impact of the Old Testament prophets? Will they see songs of Zion, Jerusalem, and Israel being lifted up to God by the church? Will they experience the glory of God upon a newly united people of God? The apostle Paul declared that the glory of God upon the Gentile church would increase so much that the Jews would want to become part of the church that they had originally spurned. (See Romans 11:11–14.)

Why not believe God for revival among the ancient people of Israel, in answer to the promises God made to their fathers?

Concerning the gospel they are enemies for your sake, but concerning the election they are beloved for the sake of the fathers. For the gifts and the calling of God are irrevocable.
(Rom. 11:28–29)

God has designed a marvelous plan of the ages to unite all things in Christ. He began with David's worshiping, praising priesthood on Mount Zion. He then universalized the worship principle to include those from all the Gentile nations who would worship Him *"in spirit and truth"* (John 4:23). And He will conclude His history of salvation by including all those who believe from His ancient people, the Jews. By the time of the end, God will have come full circle. He will have caught up earth into the heavenlies and brought heaven to earth as well. His prophetic promises will have had a dual fulfillment in both the spiritual and the natural realm at the same time. What began in David's day will then unite all men and women of faith in all generations, both Jew and Gentile, in glorious worship around the throne of God!

> *That in the dispensation of the fullness of the times He might gather together in one all things in Christ, both which are in heaven and which are on earth; in Him.*
> (Eph. 1:10)

When Paul saw this complete purpose of God for all of human history, all he could do was exclaim:

> *Oh, the depth of the riches both of the wisdom and knowledge of God! How unsearchable are His judgments and His ways past finding out!* (Rom. 11:33)

Chapter 8

It All Began with David

O f all the special emphases of the Spirit recorded in the New Testament, none predominated like the ministry of worship and praise. Possibly due to the fact that the only records that have survived from the days of the early church are the books and letters written by the apostles, we have tended to view church services in New Testament days as consisting mainly of sermons, teaching, and expository preaching. If only we had their praise and worship tapes! For certainly, the meetings of the early Christians were characterized by much singing to the Lord.

Yet this fact is seldom realized today because we tend to incorrectly assume that the early church had services similar to our own. In many Protestant traditions, the highlight of the worship service is not corporate worship at all, but the sermon, which occupies the majority of time, while the brief song service is viewed as merely a warm-up for the message. Comments are often heard, such as, "Well, it's time to stop singing now and get to the Word." Such a statement would have been incomprehensible to the early Christians, who viewed the Word of Christ as powerfully active during praise and worship. The apostle Paul taught that teaching and admonition actually occurred in the ministry of singing to the Lord:

> *Let the word of Christ dwell in you richly in all wisdom, teaching and admonishing one another* [not just in sermons, seminars, and classes, but] *in psalms and hymns and spiritual songs, singing with grace in your hearts to the Lord.* (Col. 3:16)

Experiencing God's Power in Worship

Music Can Teach God's Word

Christians in the Western world need to understand how musical intonation, chanting, and singing were linked in biblical days with the memorization and impartation of the Word of God. When the Lord wanted the children of Israel to remember a prophetic word of judgment concerning future disobedience, He instructed Moses to put the message in the form of a song and then teach the song to the people:

> *Now therefore, write down this song for yourselves, and teach it to the children of Israel; put it in their mouths, that this song may be a witness for Me against the children of Israel.* (Deut. 31:19)

Is it difficult for us to conceive of Moses as a songwriter? *"Therefore Moses wrote this song the same day, and taught it to the children of Israel"* (v. 22). This was quite an accomplishment. The song covers forty-seven verses (see Deuteronomy 32:1–47) and was written in a day, illustrating the fact that musical ability was a part of Moses' ministry. It also characterized the ministry of other great men of the Bible, notably the prophets. King David declared, *"Your statutes have been my songs"* (Ps. 119:54), indicating that his way of hiding God's word in his heart was to put it to music.

Rev. Steve Griffing has researched the relationship between Jewish chanting and the reading of Scripture. The following statement by Rabbi Johana'ah in the Jewish Talmud underscores the importance of singing the Word of God:

> If one reads the Scripture without a melody or repeats the Mishna without a tune, of him the Scripture says, *"Therefore I also gave them up to statutes that were not good"* (Ezek. 20:25). (Fischer and Griffing 1985, 36)

Today, in Jewish religious life, the readers of Scripture are still called cantors, meaning *singers*; and in the Hebrew Old Testament, scribal notations were added to the scriptural text to indicate tonal inflections and accents to be used in the singing,

80

or cantillation, of Scripture. Such singing of the Word of God has been described by Alfred Sendry, in *Music in Ancient Israel*, as a "rhythmic articulation and melodious inflection of the spoken word" (Fischer and Griffing 1985, 36).

Thirteen of the psalms are specifically described by the Hebrew word *maschil*, meaning "a psalm or song to teach or instruct." This word comes from the Hebrew verb *sakal*, which means "to instruct, to teach, to make to understand, to make wise, and to be intelligent."

The apostle Paul therefore stood squarely in the Hebraic biblical tradition when he instructed the Christian church to teach and admonish *"one another in psalms and hymns and spiritual songs"* (Col. 3:16).

BE FILLED WITH THE SPIRIT

Not only was praise and worship integrally linked in the New Testament with the impartation of the Word of God, but it was also the means of being continuously filled with the Holy Spirit.

> *And do not be drunk with wine, in which is dissipation; but be filled with the Spirit, speaking to one another in psalms and hymns and spiritual songs, singing and making melody in your heart to the Lord.* (Eph. 5:18–19)

What a refreshing way to be filled with the Holy Spirit and to stay filled! We often try so hard to achieve this by other means, to the exclusion of praise and worship. In Pentecostal traditions, we work hard with people in aggressive prayer to either get them filled or keep them filled with the Holy Spirit. In fundamental and evangelical circles, we try so diligently to teach people into this experience, to cause them to realize by faith that they have the fullness of God's Spirit.

Now it is certainly true that both teaching and prayer are important in the life of each Christian, for our reception of the Holy Spirit's fullness is definitely based upon our faith generated by the Word of God and upon our relationship with the Lord established in prayer. But in addition to these functions of teaching and prayer, we would do well in our churches to introduce the New Testament practice of praise and worship as the vehicle of being continuously *"filled with the Spirit"* as we speak to each other in *"psalms and hymns and spiritual songs."*

PRAISE AND PROPHECY

With astounding results, churches across the earth today are rediscovering this biblical connection between praise and worship and the fullness of the Holy Spirit. As rivers of the Holy Spirit are being released through worshiping congregations, not only is the *"word of Christ"* (Col. 3:16) dwelling richly in the churches, not only are the members continuing to stay *"filled with the Spirit"* (Eph. 5:18–19), but an awesome manifestation of the prophetic presence of God is also being experienced in many congregations as in the days of the early church.

The Spirit of God is bringing forth new choruses and prophetic songs in the midst of worship. Creative, fresh things are occurring in church services, as God is restoring true biblical liberty in worship and praise and is once again manifesting His divine prophetic presence. We are learning that there is an integral connection between musical praise and worship and the scriptural manifestation of prophecy.

This association between prophecy and musical or instrumental praise is seldom understood by biblical scholars and expository preachers who have had little or no musical training in their preparation for the ministry; therefore, they have no appreciation of how often in Scripture musical praise and prophecy are part of the same river of God flowing in His people.

How far we have departed from the biblical practice of singing the Scriptures! The importance of musical training was clearly understood by the Protestant reformers, most of whom were prolific songwriters. Rev. Griffing cites the following remarkable quotes from Martin Luther, which make this point unmistakably clear:

I have always loved music. Those who have mastered this art are made of good stuff, and are fit for any task. It is necessary indeed that music be taught in the schools. A teacher must be able to sing; otherwise I will not so much as look at him.   (Fischer and Griffing 1985, 42)

Next to the word of God, only music deserves being extolled as the mistress and governess of human feelings...through the medium of music the Holy Spirit placed His gifts in the hands of the prophets; again through music the devil was driven away, as was the case with Saul.   (42)

When natural music is sharpened and polished by art, then one begins to see with amazement the great and perfect wisdom of God...where one voice takes a simple part and round it sing three, four, or five other voices, leaping and springing round about, marvelously gracing the simple part, like a square-dance in heaven with friendly bows, embracings, and hearty swinging of partners.   (42)

"Through the medium of music the Holy Spirit placed His gifts in the hands of the prophets," Luther declared. As we open the Scriptures with this key of understanding, new vistas emerge that highlight the priority of praise and worship in bringing forth prophetic manifestations of the Spirit of God.

The most obvious case in point is the psalm itself. The Hebrew word for psalm, *mizmor,* means "instrumental music" and, by implication, "a poem set to musical notes." The word comes from the Hebrew verb *zamar,* meaning "to strike, touch, or play the strings of a musical instrument," hence, "to celebrate in song and music."

Interestingly, the Psalms is the most prophetic portion of Scripture, quoted more times directly and indirectly in the New Testament than any other book. As the musicians and singers in the tabernacle of David worshiped and praised the Lord *"continually before the ark"* (1 Chron. 16:4, 6 KJV), the prophetic Spirit of God came upon them and prophesied through them in an unprecedented way. An awesome stream of revelation was imparted to them, as is evidenced by the detailed prophetic pictures of the crucifixion of Christ, which were prophesied by David and his singers a thousand years before they occurred. In fact, the minutest details of the Crucifixion were so clearly re-vealed to the psalmists in the days of David, it was as if they had been standing on Calvary's hill a thousand years later:

My God, My God, why have You forsaken Me?

(Ps. 22:1)

They pierced My hands and My feet.

(v. 16)

They divide My garments among them, and for My cloth-ing they cast lots. (v. 18)

For my thirst they gave me vinegar to drink.

(Ps. 69:21)

He guards all his bones; not one of them is broken.

(Ps. 34:20)

What an intimate relationship the Lord had with the wor-shipers in David's tabernacle! Their outpouring of praise and worship brought them so close to the heart of God that He could not refrain from singing through them prophetically the very heart cry and suffering that He knew His Son would have to en-dure on Calvary. He prophesied through them in order to share with them all the poignant drama of this great event, which in the heart of God had already occurred although it was still a thousand years in the future, and He sang about it in the pro-phetic psalms of Zion. The Spirit of God not only shared the in-timate details of the Crucifixion with the worshipers in David's day but also prophesied of other matters close to the heart of the Father, such as the ultimate triumph of the people of God over all their enemies and the worldwide reign of God's king-dom.

This wealth of prophetic insight in the Psalms and its ful-fillment in the New Testament is not fully appreciated until one studies the link between the Greek version of the Old Testa-ment, the Septuagint, and the Greek New Testament. Nestle's version of the Greek New Testament contains in bold type ac-tual verbatim copies of phrases from the Greek Old Testament, the Septuagint, which were used in all the New Testament books. These quoted phrases from the Greek Old Testament in the New Testament establish many links that are not obvious in the English Bible, because their precise match disappeared when the Hebrew Old Testament and the Greek New Testament were independently translated into English.

By counting both direct quotes and indirect quotes from the Greek Old Testament in the appendix of Nestle's Greek New Testament, it is clear that the book of Psalms is the book quoted most often in the New Testament, as the following chart indicates, arranged in descending order of total quotes:

Source	Direct Quotes	Indirect Quotes	Total
Psalms	55	239	294
Isaiah	51	233	284
Genesis	20	118	138
Exodus	26	93	119
Daniel	2	96	98
Deuteronomy	42	54	96
Ezekiel	2	79	81
Jeremiah	9	64	73
Zechariah	3	39	42
Leviticus	14	24	38
Proverbs	4	26	30
Numbers	2	21	23
Hosea	6	11	17
Joel	2	12	14
Malachi	4	9	13
2 Kings	1	10	11
Job	1	10	11
1 Samuel	0	9	9
2 Samuel	5	4	9
1 Kings	0	9	9
Micah	2	7	9
Habakkuk	2	5	7
Amos	2	4	6
Joshua	1	5	6

Zephaniah	0	4	4
Judges	0	2	2
Jonah	0	1	1
Obadiah	0	1	1
Nahum	0	1	1
Lamentations	0	1	1
1 Chronicles	0	1	1
2 Chronicles	0	1	1
Esther	0	1	1
Haggai	1	0	1
Nehemiah	0	1	1
Ecclesiastes	0	0	0
Ruth	0	0	0
Song of Songs	0	0	0
Ezra	0	0	0

(Nestle 1960, 658–671)

Truly the book of Psalms outranks all other Old Testament books when it comes to prophetic usage and fulfillment in the New Testament. This is a testimony to the manifestation of the prophetic presence of God, whose Spirit moved upon the worshipers in the tabernacle of David and sang through them. Because King David so valued the prophetic presence of God that was manifest during praise and worship, he specifically appointed singers and musicians to prophesy upon their instruments in the new tabernacle that he built on Mount Zion to house the ark of the covenant. We read about this prophetic priesthood of praise in 1 Chronicles 25:1–7:

> *Moreover David and the captains of the army separated for the service some of the sons of Asaph, of Heman, and of Jeduthun...who prophesied with a harp to give thanks and to praise the LORD....All these were the sons of Heman the king's seer in the words of God, to exalt his horn....So the number of them, with their brethren who were instructed in the songs of the LORD, all who were skillful, was two hundred and eighty-eight.* (vv. 1, 3, 5, 7)

Singers and musicians were appointed to prophesy in songs of praise and worship, and the prophets themselves commanded that it should be that way.

It All Began with David

And he [Hezekiah] *stationed the Levites in the house of the LORD with cymbals, with stringed instruments, and with harps, according to the commandment of David, of Gad the king's seer, and of Nathan the prophet; for thus was the commandment of the LORD by his prophets. The Levites stood with the instruments of David, and the priests with the trumpets....And when the burnt offering began, the song of the LORD also began, with the trumpets and with the instruments of David king of Israel. So all the assembly worshiped, the singers sang, and the trumpeters sounded.*   (2 Chron. 29:25–28)

DAVIDIC PRAISE PROMOTES REVIVAL

It is important to note that in times of revival after the days of David, the kings of Judah did not feel that Davidic praise and worship was optional or was to be left to chance; they commanded it to be restored! For them, the restoration of Davidic praise was associated with the return to Israel of the divine presence of God and the prophetic anointing:

Moreover King Hezekiah and the leaders commanded the Levites to sing praise to the LORD with the words of David and of Asaph the seer. So they sang praises with gladness, and they bowed their heads and worshiped.   (v. 30)

What a prophetic move began in the worship services of the tabernacle of David on Mount Zion! What a divine manifestation of the Spirit of God! What a contrast to the repetitive singing of the same old songs in Christian circles today! David cried out in Psalm 40:3: *"He has put a new song in my mouth; praise to our God; many will see it and fear, and will trust in the LORD."* And his praising priesthood was exhorted in Psalm 33:3: *"Sing to Him a new song; play skillfully with a shout of joy."* These new songs were a foretaste of the spiritual songs or songs of the Spirit that would be sung out in the Christian church a thousand years later.

The prophetic presence of God associated with musical praise actually produced healing in David's ministry. When he was asked to sing to the Lord upon his harp, the divine power of

87

God in his ministry actually drove away oppressive evil spirits from King Saul: *"David would take a harp and play it with his hand. Then Saul would become refreshed and well, and the distressing spirit would depart from him"* (1 Sam. 16:23).

SAUL ENABLED TO PROPHESY

The prophetic anointing expressed in praise and worship was also evident in Israel's history during the days of Samuel, the prophet who laid hands on David and imparted to him the anointing of the Holy Spirit. In those days, mobile ministry teams of musician–prophets traveled throughout Israel, worshiping and prophesying the Word of the Lord. The prophetic atmosphere was so great that King Saul, coming in contact with them, was himself enabled to prophesy.

> *You will meet a group of prophets coming down from the high place with a stringed instrument, a tambourine, a flute, and a harp before them; and they will be prophesying. Then the Spirit of the LORD will come upon you* [Saul], *and you will prophesy with them and be turned into another man.* (1 Sam. 10:5–6)

ANOINTED MUSIC ASSISTS ELISHA

Musical praise and prophecy were also associated in the ministry of Elisha, the man anointed with the double portion of God's Spirit. In the presence of two ungodly kings and a backslidden one, in whose presence he was asked to prophesy, even this great man required anointed music before he could receive a prophetic word:

> *And Elisha said..."Were it not that I regard the presence of Jehoshaphat king of Judah, I would not look at you, nor see you. But now bring me a musician." Then it happened, when the musician played, that the hand of the LORD came upon him. And he said, "Thus says the LORD."* (2 Kings 3:14–16)

OTHER PROPHETIC SONGS

Would prophetic ministries today even think of asking for anointed musicians when it is time to prophesy? They certainly did in biblical times. A significant amount of Old Testament prophecy was apparently sung in musical form. Chapter twelve of Isaiah seems to have been one such prophetic song, for the prophet declares: *"The LORD JEHOVAH is my strength and my song....Sing unto the LORD; for he hath done excellent things"* (vv. 2, 5 KJV).

Did Ezekiel also prophesy in song and play a musical instrument? Quite possibly, for the Lord said to him,

> *Indeed you are to them as a very lovely song of one who has a pleasant voice and can play well on an instrument; for they hear your words, but they do not do them.*
> (Ezek. 33:32)

The third chapter of Habakkuk was a prophetic prayer set to music, for it was written for *"the Chief Musician. With my stringed instruments"* (Hab. 3:19).

In the New Testament, the association between praise and worship and the gift of prophecy is also clearly seen. It was in an atmosphere of worship in the church at Antioch that the prophetic word of the Lord was spoken to Barnabas and Paul, sending them out on their first missionary journey:

> *As they ministered to the Lord and fasted, the Holy Spirit said, "Now separate to Me Barnabas and Saul for the work to which I have called them." Then, having fasted and prayed, and laid hands on them, they sent them away.*
> (Acts 13:2–3)

The word *ministered* in verse two is the Greek word *leitourgeo*, from which we get our English word *liturgy*. The word definitely involves the meaning of worship. Thus, the verse could be interpreted, "As they worshiped the Lord...the Holy Spirit said prophetically, '*Separate to Me Barnabas and Saul.*'"

Experiencing God's Power in Worship

THE EFFECTS OF PROPHECY

One of the most outstanding characteristics of the early church was the awesome prophetic presence of God that was manifested in their worship services. This prophetic atmosphere was so powerful that unbelievers would come into the meetings, and in the midst of worship and the manifestation of spiritual gifts, the prophetic word spoken in the church would actually expose the secrets of their hearts. They would cry out that God was there and would begin participating in the worship service:

> *If all prophesy, and an unbeliever or an uninformed person comes in, he is convinced by all, he is convicted by all. And thus the secrets of his heart are revealed; and so, falling down on his face, he will worship God and report that God is truly among you.* (1 Cor. 14:24–25)

Churches are beginning to see these same results today, as they are experiencing a mighty restoration of prophetic anointing. This manifestation of God's prophetic word in worship services is actually having the same evangelistic impact now as it did in Corinth.

Even in Old Testament times, King David knew well the magnetic impact of prophetic new songs sung spontaneously in worship. David wrote: *"He has put a new song in my mouth; praise to our God; many will see it* [the new song] *and fear, and will trust in the LORD"* (Ps. 40:3).

In the early church, the apostle Paul placed spontaneous songs first on the list of prophetic manifestations. These songs exposed the hearts of unbelievers and brought them to Christ:

> *And so, falling down on his face, he will worship God and report that God is truly among you. How is it then, brethren? Whenever you come together, each of you has a psalm.* (1 Cor. 14:25–26)

The *"word of Christ"* (Col. 3:16), which is to dwell richly in us as we teach and admonish *"one another in psalms and hymns and spiritual songs"* (v. 16), definitely includes the prophetic word of Christ, which is being sung today in the church just as in the days of old. These glorious, spontaneous spiritual songs or songs of the Spirit open the hearts of men to the powerful presence of the living God.

HEAVENLY SONGS ARE BEING HEARD

God Himself is singing though His people today. Songs from the very throne of heaven are penetrating the veil, or the separation between heaven and earth, and are being heard in the church.

> *The LORD your God in your midst, The Mighty One, will save; He will rejoice over you with gladness, He will quiet you with His love, He will rejoice over you with singing.*
> (Zeph. 3:17)

The Lord Himself sings out in the midst of the congregation and testifies to us through His prophetic word. *"For the testimony of Jesus is the spirit of prophecy"* (Rev. 19:10). Portions of His prophetic messages to at least seven churches are found in the second and third chapters of Revelation: *"He who has an ear, let him hear what the Spirit says to the churches"* (Rev. 3:22). Jesus is still testifying in the church today by speaking through the gift of prophecy.

The apostle Paul recognized the importance of prophetic ministry in the church and especially encouraged the churches to speak and sing of the word of the Lord prophetically in their services:

> *Pursue love, and desire spiritual gifts, but especially that you may prophesy....He who prophesies speaks edification and exhortation and comfort to men....For you can all prophesy one by one, that all may learn and all may be encouraged.*
> (1 Cor. 14:1, 3, 31)

The Scriptures also teach us that Jesus Himself sings praise through the church to the Father. The author of Hebrews quoted Psalm 22:22 and applied it to Jesus Christ:

> *For both He who sanctifies and those who are being sancti-*
> *fied are all of one, for which reason He is not ashamed to*
> *call them brethren, saying, "I [Jesus] will declare Your*
> *name to My brethren; in the midst of the assembly I will*
> *sing praise to You."*   (Heb. 2:11–12)

What an exalted view of the prophetic song is found in Scripture! The Lord Himself is speaking, testifying, and singing prophetically in the midst of His people. His voice is truly sounding out in power and great glory in this present generation through the church, which is His body on earth.

Chapter 9

Restoring God's Glory
to the Church

I f only the power and glory of the presence of the Lord in the early church could have continued through the centuries to the present day! What a marvelous, continuous history of the book of Acts could have been compiled by now! Imagine chapter upon chapter being added to the exploits of the first-century church.

But as one scans the history of the Christian church, just the opposite has occurred. Instead of the continuous creative flow of the Holy Spirit infusing life, gifts, and spontaneity into Christian worship, one finds over the centuries of Christian history an inexorably strong trend toward standardization, uniformity, rituals, and liturgical repetition. It is as if the opposite of what happened in Israel's history has occurred in the Christian church: the traditional, ceremonial, ritualistic religion of the tabernacle of Moses has grown stronger, and the spontaneous, liberating, joyful, prophetic praise and worship of the tabernacle of David in Zion has diminished.

A REVERSE EVOLUTION

After the first generation of New Testament apostles perished, the powerful moving of the Holy Spirit in signs and wonders and in prophetic liberty in worship began to wane; and, after many centuries of Christian evolution, we find Christian priests acting in a very similar fashion to the Mosaic, Levitical order, as they moved backward from the prophetic liberty of early Christian worship to follow specifically prescribed, never varying patterns of ceremonial observances, such as the lighting of candles, the burning of incense, setting out unleavened bread, cleansing themselves in the water of sanctification, and such. It was as if the Christian church, which had begun in the prophetic atmosphere that characterized Davidic worship during the days of the Psalms, actually regressed to the ceremonial rituals similar to those of the Levitical priesthood under the Old Testament.

Obviously, such a radical shift in Christianity did not happen in a day or even in a century. In the second century of Christian history, we find that prophetic gifts were still in action as seen in the following excerpt from a letter from Ignatius, bishop of the church in Antioch, to the church in Philadelphia:

> When I was with you I cried out, raising my voice—it was God's voice—"Pay heed to the bishop, the presbytery, and the deacons." It was the Spirit that kept on preaching in these words, "Do nothing apart from the bishop; keep your bodies as if they were God's temple; value unity; flee schism." (Richardson 1970, 109–10)

Indeed, throughout church history, there has always existed a thread of charismatic gifts, as demonstrated in the book *They Speak in Other Tongues* by Rev. Larry Christensen (1968).

But the point to be made here is that these gifts of the Holy Spirit slowly became limited to individuals, some of whom stood out so markedly against the spiritual lifelessness of the church at large that they were actually granted sainthood. However, such movings of the Spirit ceased to be permitted in the public, corporate worship of the church.

CONFORMITY SQUELCHED CREATIVITY

Undoubtedly, it was the standardization of Christian worship that ultimately ruled out the spontaneous moving of the Spirit of God. The church fathers obviously had reasons for each step they took in the direction of uniformity and conformity, but the end result was to ignore the very power of the Holy Spirit

94

that had given birth to the church in the first place. In its desire to unify the church on an empire-wide scale in the face of heretical and sectarian attacks on its orthodoxy during the first three to six centuries of its existence, the church rallied to codify and standardize Christian worship and doctrine across the Roman Empire. Ceremonies and creeds, and the liturgy of the worship service itself, became entirely predefined, agreed on in advance by church councils. No one was ever expected to do or say anything other than what was prescribed; thus no one ever did.

What a departure from the glorious, creative spontaneity of worship services in Bible times! Who could cry anymore with the psalmist David: *"He has put a new song in my mouth; praise to our God; many will see it* [the new song] *and fear, and will trust in the LORD"* (Ps. 40:3)? Who could conceive anymore of worship services open to the moving of the Holy Spirit, as in the days of the New Testament?

> *If all prophesy, and an unbeliever or an uninformed person comes in, he is convinced by all, he is convicted by all. And thus the secrets of his heart are revealed; and so, falling down on his face, he will worship God and report that God is truly among you. How is it then, brethren? Whenever you come together, each of you has a psalm, has a teaching, has a tongue, has a revelation, has an interpretation. Let all things be done for edification....Let two or three prophets speak, and let the others judge. But if anything is revealed to another who sits by, let the first keep silent. For you can all prophesy one by one, that all may learn and all may be encouraged.* (1 Cor. 14:24–26, 29–31)

How far the church strayed from its glorious, Spirit-filled beginning! The heavens were closed off and sealed up tight. Gone was the prophetic anointing that had opened up things *"in the heavenly places in Christ Jesus"* (Eph. 2:6) and had revealed them to the church on earth. Gone were the visions of the seers of both Old and New Testaments, who saw things in the Spirit and declared them to the people of God. No opportunity existed anymore, as in the days of David, Solomon, and the New Testament church, for God to move sovereignly and creatively by the

Holy Spirit, manifesting His gifts and His songs within the openness granted Him in the worship services of His people.

What a tragedy! Could biblical liberty in worship ever occur again? Could God ever again move through His body on earth as He had previously done in biblical times? Even considering the Protestant Reformation and the centuries that followed, one looks largely in vain for evidence of Christian worship services in which the windows were thrown open to fresh breezes of the Holy Spirit and to the spontaneous creativity of a divine infusion of life and gifts into the meetings. To be sure, important doctrinal truths of Scripture were recovered, such as the foundational understandings of justification by faith, sanctification, and the absolute authority of the Bible. Elements of the liturgies of worship were altered to reflect the application of Reformation truth to the different state churches of Europe—Lutheran churches in Germany, Presbyterian churches in Switzerland, Episcopal churches in England, Reformed churches in Holland (to describe these denominations by their American counterparts)—and these services of worship were rendered more intelligible to the congregations, being conducted in the language of the people and containing elements of practical Bible teaching for daily living.

But one central fact remained unchanged following the first few centuries of Christian history: the order of the worship service itself remained essentially predetermined, in many cases written and decided on in advance by the liturgical committees of ecclesiastical church councils. In no way was the Spirit of the Lord allowed to have free course to reveal Himself directly to His body, the church. In no way were the windows of heaven opened to allow a Davidic or a New Testament emphasis on prophetic spontaneity in worship.

REVIVAL FIRES AMONG THE MORAVIANS

A few notable exceptions to this rule exist. One refreshing example occurred in the life of a little known church of the Moravian Brethren in northern Germany in the early 1700s. A German landlord, Count Zinzendorf, had permitted a group of several hundred exiled Christians to settle on his estate in

Herrnhut in northern Germany. They were fleeing severe persecutions in the southern province of Bavaria.

Impressed with the piety and devotion of this transplanted Brethren congregation, Count Zinzendorf, who himself had converted to Christ as a young child, eventually became the leader of this band of believers. In August 1727, this small church experienced an outpouring of the Holy Spirit that not only transformed their own lives, but also opened the door to the modern Protestant missionary movement and transformed the nation of England through the ministries of two of their converts, John and Charles Wesley. Read the following beautiful description of this revival from one of its historians:

> Truly the great Moravian revival of 1727...was preceded and followed by the most extraordinary praying.
>
> July 16. The Count poured forth his soul in a heart-affecting prayer, accompanied by a flood of tears; this prayer produced an extraordinary effect....Not only Count Zinzendorf, but many other brethren also began to pray as never before.
>
> July 22. A number of Brethren covenanted together of their own accord, engaging to meet often...to pour out their hearts in prayer and hymns.
>
> August 5. The Count spent the whole night in watching, in company of about twelve or fourteen brethren. At midnight there was held on the Hutberg a large meeting for the purpose of prayer, at which great emotion prevailed.
>
> August 10. About noon, while Pastor Rothe was holding the meeting at Herrnhut, he felt himself overwhelmed by a wonderful and irresistible power of the Lord, and sank down into the dust before God, and with him sank down the whole assembled congregation in an ecstasy of feeling. In this frame of mind they continued till midnight engaged in prayer, singing, weeping and supplication.   (Greenfield 1931, 27–28)

The actual outpouring of the Holy Spirit occurred on August 13, 1727, and was described as follows:

> God says, "It shall come to pass—I will pour." This was His promise through the prophet Joel. This first

fulfillment of this promise was on the Day of Pentecost. There is nothing in the New Testament to indicate that this was to be the one and only fulfillment of this promise. On the contrary, we read in the book of Acts of many outpourings of the Holy Spirit, as in Samaria, as in Ephesus, and even in the case of the Gentiles.

And verily the thirteenth of August 1727 was a day of the outpouring of the Holy Spirit. We saw the hand of God and His wonders, and we were all under the cloud of our fathers baptized with their Spirit. The Holy Ghost came upon us and in those days great signs and wonders took place in our midst....A great hunger after the Word of God took possession of us so that we had to have three services every day, viz. 5 and 7:30 a.m. and 9 p.m.

(Greenfield 1931, 14–16)

Incredible! A moving of God's Spirit came upon a church so clearly and powerfully that portions of the service were actually initiated and directed by the Spirit of the Lord. Something wonderfully new was happening. Testimonies and reports about this Moravian Brethren Revival reveal unprecedented expressions of the creative moving of the Spirit of God, producing extemporaneous new songs as they prophesied and sang by direct inspiration of the Spirit, just as in the days of David and the New Testament church:

Christian women and young people also were filled with the Holy Spirit and prophesied. Their prayers and praises often found expression in psalms and hymns and spiritual songs....A truly converted [person]...when he is baptized with the Holy Ghost and with fire often breaks out into sacred song and it is generally prayer or praise addressed to Jesus. (Greenfield 1931, 57, 60)

Moravian believers learned to release themselves to the creativity of the Holy Spirit. They found that this direct leading of the Spirit could be trusted to bring forth something beautiful and awe-inspiring:

A blessed meeting of the children took place in the evening of the 26th of August, and on the 29th, from the hours of ten o'clock at night until one the following morning...the girls...spent these hours in praying, singing and weeping...The boys were at the same time engaged in earnest prayer in another place.

Was there ever in the whole of church history such an astonishing prayer-meeting as that which, beginning in 1727, went on one hundred years? It is something absolutely unique. It was known as the "Hourly Intercession," and it meant that by relays of brethren and sisters prayer without ceasing was made to God for all the work and wants of His church.

(Greenfield 1931, 28–30, 57)

This incredible spiritual awakening among the Moravians was no mere blowing in and out of the Holy Spirit with a lot of heavenly excitement and few earthly results. Quite the contrary! All the earmarks were there of a genuine, world-shaking revival. Look what occurred:

During the first three decades after their spiritual Pentecost, they carried the Gospel of salvation by the blood of the Lamb not only to nearly every country in Europe, but also to many pagan races in America, North and South, Asia and Africa. Their first mission was to the Negroes in the West Indies, five years after the outpouring of the Spirit....So generally has the leadership of the Moravian church in Foreign Missions been recognized, that the well-known German historian of Protestant missions, Dr. Warneck, testifies: "This small church in twenty years called into being more missions than the whole Evangelical church has done in two centuries."

Fifty years before the beginning of modern Foreign Missions by William Carey, the Moravian Church had led the way into pagan countries both by precept and example. Their English missionary magazine, Periodical Accounts, inspired Dr. Carey, in a meeting of his Baptist brethren he threw a copy of the paper on a table with these memorable and historic words:

"See what the Moravians have done! Cannot we follow their example and in obedience to our Heavenly

99

Master go out into the world, and preach the Gospel to the heathen?

From that one small village community more than one hundred missionaries went out in twenty-five years. You will look in vain elsewhere for anything to match it."

(Greenfield 1931, 18–19, 30)

Not only were nations reached with the Gospel through their own missionaries, but also the Moravians were indirectly responsible for bringing to birth the Great Awakening in England, which came to pass through the ministries of two of their most notable converts, John and Charles Wesley.

THE GREAT AWAKENING

It was the power of God evident in the lives of some Moravian missionaries that first arrested the attention of a young graduate of Oxford University, the Rev. John Wesley. He was on a ship with them in passage to the colony of Georgia, where they were all going as missionaries. During the journey, a terrible storm struck the ship. The mainsail split, water poured in between the decks, and in the midst of this catastrophe, Wesley found the Moravians down in the hold of the ship singing psalms and praising the Lord, with no evidence of any fear in their hearts. Wesley was impressed. His diary records the following:

A terrible screaming began among the English. The Germans [Moravian missionaries]...calmly sang on. I asked one of them afterwards, "Were you not afraid?" He answered, "I thank God, no."...This was the most glorious day which I have hitherto seen. (Parker 1974, 36).

After their arrival in Georgia, Mr. Spangenberg, one of the Moravian missionaries, put his finger on Wesley's condition:

"Do you know Jesus Christ?"

I paused, and said, "I know He is the Saviour of the world."

"True," replied he, "but do you know He has saved you?"

I answered, "I hope He has died to save me."

He only added, "Do you know yourself?"
I said, "I do." But I fear they were vain words.
(Parker 1974, 36–37)

This outpouring of God's Spirit that breathed life and creativity into their services of worship and prayer also took the
Moravians to the ends of the earth with the Gospel of salvation.
These Moravian missionaries pursued people relentlessly until
they capitulated and gave themselves over to Christ as Lord.
Even John Wesley could not escape their persistence. They followed him back to England and brought many people who testified to him of having experienced an instantaneous conversion
by the power of Christ. His diary records the following:

> I could not understand...how a man could at once be
> thus turned from darkness to light, from sin and misery
> to righteousness and joy in the Holy Ghost. I searched the
> Scriptures again...but, to my utter astonishment, found
> scarce any instances there of other than instantaneous
> conversions.
> I had but one retreat left; namely, "Thus, I grant,
> God wrought in the first ages of Christianity; but the
> times are changed...." But on Sunday the 23rd, I was beat
> out of this retreat too, by the concurring evidence of
> several living witnesses (brought to Wesley by the
> Moravians); who testified God had thus wrought in
> themselves, giving them in a moment such a faith in the
> blood of His Son as translated them out of darkness into
> light....Here ended my disputing. I could now only cry out,
> "Lord, help thou my unbelief." (April 22–23, 1738)
> (Curnock 1909–1916, 454–6)

The Lord did help his unbelief. The next month, Wesley
attended a worship service of the Moravian community in London, and it was in this meeting that God visited him and
changed his heart, and thereby a nation.

> In the evening I went very unwillingly [possibly pressed
> by his Moravian friends?] to a society in Aldersgate Street,
> where one was reading Luther's preface to the Epistle to

the Romans. About a quarter before nine, while he was describing the change which God works in the heart through faith in Christ, I felt my heart strangely warmed. I felt I did trust in Christ, Christ alone for salvation; and an assurance was given me that He had taken away my sins, even mine, and saved me from the law of sin and death.   (Curnock 1909–1916, 472–9)

We have seen in this revival among the Moravian Brethren the full circle of God's intended blessings for His church. As on the Day of Pentecost, the Holy Spirit descended on them from *"on high"* (Luke 24:49), from the realm of the heavenlies, and blew on them powerfully and prophetically, causing them to hear the melodies of heaven and the word of the Lord. This same Spirit then took them out into the world to save and transform it.

But you shall receive power when the Holy Spirit has come upon you; and you shall be witnesses to Me in Jerusalem, and in all Judea and Samaria, and to the end of the earth.
(Acts 1:8)

The mighty power of God born in John Wesley through the ministry of the Moravians didn't stop there. It swept through England in dramatic fashion, blowing right out of the Anglican churches, who rejected it, and into the fields and streets. Wesley was introduced to preaching in the open air by George Whitefield, an evangelist from America:

In the evening I reached Bristol and met Mr. Whitefield there. I could scarcely reconcile myself at first to this strange way of preaching in the fields....I had been all my life (till very lately) so tenacious of every point relating to decency and order that I should have thought the saving of souls almost a sin if it had not been done in a church.
(March 29, 1739)   (Parker 1974, 67–68)

As if to confirm John Wesley in his open-air preaching, the power of God greatly impacted the hearers, as people physically responded.

I had an opportunity to talk with him [George Whitefield] of those outward signs which had so often accompanied the inward work of God....The next day he had an opportunity of informing himself better: for no sooner had he begun [in the application of his sermon] to invite all sinners to believe in Christ, than four persons sank down close to him, almost in the same moment. One of them lay without either sense or motion. A second trembled exceedingly....The fourth, equally convulsed, called on God with strong cries and tears. From this time, I trust, we shall all suffer God to carry on His own work in the way that pleaseth Him. (July 7, 1739)   (Parker 1974, 76)

I preached on the righteousness of the law and the righteousness of faith. While I was speaking, several dropped down as dead and among the rest such a cry was heard of sinners groaning for the righteousness of faith as almost drowned my voice. But many of these soon lifted up their heads with joy and broke out in thanksgiving. (June 12, 1742)   (Parker 1974, 99)

Just one Sunday schedule in the ministry of John Wesley serves to underscore the tremendous response of the people to his outdoor preaching:

At seven in the morning I preached to about a thousand persons at Bristol, and afterward to about fifteen hundred on the top of Hannam Mount in Kingswood....About five thousand were in the afternoon at Rose Green among whom I stood and cried in the name of the Lord...at five in the afternoon I was at a little society in the Back Lane. (April 8, 1739)   (Parker 1974, 68)

As the Sundays progressed, the crowds grew:

I declared to about ten thousand, what they must do to be saved. My mother went with us, about five, to Kennington, where were supposed to be twenty thousand people. I again insisted on that foundation of all our hope, "Believe in the Lord Jesus, and thou shalt be saved." (September 9, 1739)

> I preached at Moorfields to about ten thousand, and at Kennington Common to, I believe, nearly twenty thousand..." (September 16, 1739)
>
> I declared to about ten thousand, in Moorfields, with great enlargement of spirit....At Kennington I enforced to about twenty thousand that great truth, "One thing is needful." (September 23, 1739)   (Parker 1974, 78–79)

The praise and the worship of the Wesleyan revival also spilled out into the open air.

> About noon we went on board. In two or three hours we reached the mouth of the harbor...about eight we began singing on the quarterdeck and soon drew all our fellow passengers, as well as the captain, with the greatest part of his men....We then spent some time in prayer. They all kneeled down with us.   (Parker 1974, 216)

John Wesley was consumed with a universal desire to preach the Word of God:

> I look upon all the world as my parish; thus far I mean, that, in whatever part of it I am, I judge it meet, right, and my bounden duty to declare unto all that are willing to hear, the glad tidings of salvation.   (Parker 1974, 74)

SOCIAL REFORM RESULTED FROM REVIVAL

John Wesley's life and ministry touched all of England. His converts and those influenced by what has since been called the Evangelical Awakening literally transformed English society. As evangelical preachers ministered in prisons, factories, and slums, they began to raise a cry for humanitarianism and justice. Prison reform laws were enacted in England. Child labor laws were passed, limiting the hours that children could work in mines and factories. Even the abolition of slavery became law in England largely through the efforts of men like Wilberforce in Parliament, who had been touched by the Evangelical Awakening and messages by John Wesley, such as the following:

> Can human law turn darkness into light or evil into good?...Right is right and wrong is wrong still...I absolutely deny all slave-holding to be consistent with any degree of even natural justice.   (Bready 1946, 142)

It can be maintained without fear of contradiction that many social reform movements, now claimed by liberal humanists, actually had their roots in evangelical, heaven-sent revivals. Shut out of the historic churches in England, the Holy Spirit had moved into the streets, the fields, the factories, and the prisons of its cities. At Wesley's death, over 135,000 converts had been organized into societies of 50 and bands of 10. The seeds of Methodism had been planted. Yet the structure of the Methodist worship that originated in these newly formed churches was still basically an adaptation of former liturgical models, with no open windows through which the Spirit of God was allowed to blow and move inside the church services.

REVIVAL IN AMERICA

With the rise of revivalism in America during the 1800s and the emergence of the popular preaching of Dwight Moody, Charles Finney, and the like, church worship music was enriched by gospel hymns and choruses, some of which have continued in use until the present day. These easy-to-learn songs lent themselves to repetitious and joyful singing and provided an exciting lift to church worship services. But still nothing spontaneous, prophetic, and creative was experienced in the flow of the services that approximated the worship flow of the tabernacle of David and the New Testament church—nothing that is, until the great Pentecostal outpouring of the Spirit of God that occurred in the early 1900s.

THE BEGINNINGS IN KANSAS

It began in such a humble, unexpected way. In Topeka, Kansas, forty students gathered in an obscure Holiness Bible School. They were seeking the baptism of the Holy Spirit they had read about in the book of Acts. For months they had been fasting and praying for the power from on high to be released in their midst. They were unaware of what was about to happen, something that would shake the modern church world to its foundations. During the watch night prayer service on New Year's Day, January 1, 1900, it happened:

> The spirit of prayer was upon us in the evening. It was nearly seven o'clock on this first day of January that it came into my heart to ask Brother Parham to lay his hands on me that I might receive the Holy Ghost. Instantly, the Holy Spirit came upon me and I began to speak in other tongues and it was clearly manifest when a new language was spoken. I had the added joy and glory my heart had longed for and a depth of the presence of the Lord such as no tongue can describe.   (Ewart 1947, 31)

This revival of the Holy Spirit outpouring spread rapidly through the city. The fire of God was beginning to burn brightly:

> Hundreds flocked to see the great sight. Prayer was held day and night, and soon the experience of Acts 2:4 was duplicated in hundreds of cases...the sick were brought from hundreds of miles away and...miracles of healing would take place.   (Ewart 1947, 32)

From Topeka, Kansas, ministers carried torches to light fires of the Holy Spirit in other cities as well—from Chicago to Houston and elsewhere. By April of 1906, the stage was set for one of the most remarkable outpourings of the Holy Spirit in the history of the church.

REVIVAL SPREADS TO AZUSA STREET

A black holiness pastor from Houston, Texas, Brother Seymour, had traveled to Los Angeles to share with a sister church there a glorious new baptism of the Holy Spirit that he and his congregation had experienced. A new Pentecost had come! God was moving in power again. Acts 2:4 was being repeated, as people were being filled with the Holy Spirit. Tongues of fire were falling upon believers, and the glory of the Lord was being experienced.

Expecting the church in Los Angeles to respond with joy and excitement, Pastor Seymour began to share his newfound enthusiasm, when—Slam!—his meetings were canceled. The church doors were shut to him, and he found himself out on the street. This church had decided to keep the windows of heaven locked up tightly!

Members of the congregation, the Asbury family, took pity on this displaced preacher and invited him to stay with them in their home for a few days, again not knowing that their house was to become the manger for another incredible visitation from heaven. What a modest beginning for a world-shaking revival! How reminiscent of the original Day of Pentecost.

After spending several days in prayer and studying the Word, one night as they were seeking the Lord together, the Holy Spirit fell on the dozen or so individuals in the Asbury home. A historian of the period describes what occurred:

> The new recipients were beside themselves with joy. They shouted and praised God for three days and nights.... People came from everywhere. By the next morning there was no way of getting near that house ....This continued until the whole city of Los Angeles was mightily stirred....During these three wonderful days hundreds of people were saved, the sick were healed, and many received the baptism with the Holy Ghost according to the scriptural pattern. Then they went out to fund themselves a church home. They were led to an idle building on Azusa Street....That meeting lasted for over three years, going on day and night without a break....The news spread far and wide that Los Angeles had been visited by a sweeping revival after the order of that which struck the world on the Day of Pentecost. (Ewart 1947, 39–40)

The heavens were being opened again. Once again, the living water of the Holy Spirit was being poured out on the earth in copious downpours. A universal move of God had begun.

It is difficult to overemphasize the magnitude of this revival. Pastors and missionaries from around the world visited the old building on Azusa Street. It became one of the most important addresses in Los Angeles. This Holy Spirit outpouring continued to burn brightly for years. Ambassadors of the Lord carried this new Pentecostal fire far and wide, even to other nations, such as Sweden, China, and Chile. Branching fires were kindled that soon spread over the whole earth, burning until this present day, so that the Pentecostal movement is now recognized by church growth specialists as the fastest growing Christian movement in the world.

What were the characteristics of this revival? A closer look reveals striking similarities to the experiences of King David and his worshiping priesthood on Mount Zion and also to the gift-endowed New Testament church, for the windows of heaven were opened up once again, and the Holy Spirit was again set free to move creatively through worshiping congregations.

Indeed, the spontaneity in the meetings was one of the most noteworthy aspects of the Azusa Street Revival. There was a free flow of worship, exhortation, preaching, and prayer. The meetings moved freely under divine guidance:

> There were no special speakers announced, and no sermon themes were ever announced, for special occasions. There were no special occasions. The unexpected invariably happened. No one knew what was coming next. What God would do. All was spontaneous, in the freedom of the Spirit....The Spirit dominated the scene....Those were Holy Ghost meetings, led of the Lord.   (Ewart 1947, 44)

And the singing! Reminiscent of the days of the Psalms and of the New Testament church, prophetic spontaneity began to occur in the praise and worship. It has been reported that trained opera stars came to the Azusa Street meetings just to watch in awe as untrained voices under the anointing of the Holy Spirit sang the finest of music. A Pentecostal historian describes what happened:

> The choir was substituted by what was called "The Heavenly Choir." This singing service was literally inspired by the Holy Ghost. It was mostly in known tunes but in words chosen by the Holy Ghost. This was perhaps

the most supernatural and amazing thing about the meetings. It was this that convicted the writer that God was in the midst....Bands of angels have been seen by those under the power of the Spirit at such times of heavenly visitation. Here was one choir without a discord.

(Ewart 1947, 40)

Prophetic psalms, hymns, and spiritual songs began to flow in the church again, as in biblical times. The Spirit of God was again set free to move through the church. Heaven once more had come down to earth, as the unseen God was made manifest through His visible body. The windows of heaven were unlocked, and a fresh breeze of the Spirit began to blow. And God loved it! As if to confirm this infant movement to the world at large, the Lord backed up the Pentecostal message by working signs and wonders, as in the days of the apostles.

THE INTENSITY DIMINISHES

It would have been wonderful if this spiritual awakening had continued unabated until the present day. Unfortunately, the contrary occurred. Over the decades that followed, the Pentecostal movement began to wane in its intensity and liberty. Several factors contributed to this spiritual decline. Different streams of churches within the Pentecostal movement began to separate themselves from one another, some along racial boundaries and others along theological ones, as various denominations were formed with their doctrinal distinctives, and hence their differences, firmly entrenched. This fostered infighting and often strong divisiveness.

Contrary to the admonition of the apostle Paul to *"keep the unity of the Spirit...till we all come to the unity of the faith"* (Eph. 4:3, 13), different groups in the Pentecostal movement evidently decided to part company and therefore to break the *"unity of the Spirit"* because they didn't have absolute *"unity of the faith."* A standardization and drive for uniformity occurred within the new denominations, as attempts were made to rule out error and wildfire by denominational directives concerning the structuring, and hence control, of worship services. As educational institutions were founded for the training of ministers, there arose an almost apologetic attitude in Pentecostal circles about the perceived excesses of unbridled expressions of liberty in worship. Rather than striving to bring a proper balance between structure and spontaneity, it became easier to simply rule out spontaneity in favor of structure. To avoid wildfire, it was simpler to put out all fires that threatened to burn out of control. To avoid the stigma of being called "Holy Rollers," it was easier to stop any spontaneous manifestations of the Holy Spirit.

As the Pentecostal movement entered the 1940s, it had already lost many of its early distinctive qualities. In many churches, no gifts or manifestations of the Spirit ever occurred. Prayer for the infilling of the Holy Spirit was often relegated to the prayer room, and then only at special occasions, such as once-a-year spiritual renewal conferences. The windows of heaven were increasingly closed off, so that the wind of the Spirit seldom blew in with power. Gone were the manifestations of the prophetic songs that had once so gloriously characterized the worship of David's tabernacle.

The body life of the New Testament church that expressed itself in supernatural charismatic gifts had all but ceased. Christian worship once again moved away from its biblical liberty, as a kind of rigor mortis set in.

How difficult it is to maintain true biblical liberty in worship! Whenever God has been allowed to break into the earthly stream of Christian worship by unusual manifestations of the Holy Spirit, it has usually been at times of great transition during the upheavals of revival. For brief intervals of time, the Holy Spirit has been given the reins and has moved with power. But inexorably, and true to form, the religious attitude of human control and conformity slowly regains the upper hand, and new life metastasizes into new form. Thus, a new tradition is born, which must be maintained with zeal and dedication in the future.

WHAT ABOUT TODAY?

We are creatures of habit. We react in the present based on the past. God is a God of the future; He acts now in the present based on where He wants to take us in the future. Those who desire to follow the Lord need to be prepared to act with Him now because of His future plans instead of reacting against Him because of past religious tradition.

When Jesus appeared, whose Word was the source of Judaism, so much religious tradition had accumulated over the centuries that He was not even recognized. Do we in the Christian church face that same danger today, when the manifestations of the power of the Holy Spirit that occurred in the early church are now appearing? Do our present-day religious traditions make room for experiencing the power of the living Christ today?

Is it possible to bring forth a theology that mandates the release of the Holy Spirit and is irrevocably committed to keeping the windows of heaven open to fresh outpourings of the Spirit of God? Can there ever be a tradition developed that encourages the manifestations of spiritual gifts, that makes room for them, fosters them, and nourishes them? Is it possible for Christian worshipers to live a lifetime under an open heaven, drinking in the living water of the Holy Spirit? Is it possible for entire generations of worshipers to enjoy the manifest presence of God, as David did during his forty-year reign and as the early church did during the time of the apostles?

In order to keep the windows of heaven open, in order to maintain revival fires for coming generations, it is necessary to rediscover the use of the *"key of David"* (Rev. 3:7).

Chapter 10

The Key of David

These things says He who is holy, He who is true, He who has
the key of David, He who opens and no one shuts, and shuts and
no one opens....See, I have set before you an open door.
—Revelation 3:7–8

David used a key that opened a doorway into the heavenly realm. That key was worshiping the Lord in spirit and in truth. By using this key, David and his priesthood on Mount Zion opened a way for themselves into the very presence of God.

Other men in Scripture knew this principle well. The apostle John said, *"I was in the Spirit on the Lord's Day"* (Rev. 1:10); being *"in the Spirit,"* his prophetic vision was activated, and he began to see and hear things in the heavenly realm. A *"door was opened in heaven"* (Rev. 4:1 KJV), and John heard a voice saying, *"Come up here, and I will show you things which must take place after this"* (Rev. 4:1). Immediately, he was *"in the Spirit"* and began to see the throne of God, the emerald rainbow, the twenty-four elders, the seven lamps of fire, the crystal sea, and multitudes of angels. (See Revelation 4–5.)

The patriarch Jacob had a similar experience. In his prophetic dream, the heavens were opened, and he saw the Lord standing above a ladder that reached from heaven to earth. He heard the Lord declare life-changing prophetic promises concerning his future. When he awoke from his prophetic dream, he declared:

"Surely the LORD is in this place, and I did not know it."
And he was afraid and said, "How awesome is this place!

113

Experiencing God's Power in Worship

This is none other than the house of God, and this is the gate of heaven!" (Gen. 28:16–17)

SPIRIT-FILLED WORSHIP

The house of God is therefore to be the gateway into the heavenlies. What a glorious characteristic of the church! The church is to experience an entrance into the heavenly realm by the ministry of the Spirit of God. No wonder Jesus told the Samaritan woman that the Father was seeking those who would worship Him *"in spirit and truth"* (John 4:24).

The Father knows that when He finds worshiping churches on earth, filled with the Holy Spirit, He can open the heavens to these congregations, and the two-way ladder between heaven and earth can begin functioning again. He can cause these churches in the Spirit to be seated with Christ in heavenly places (Eph. 2:6), and He can also bring His power and glory down to earth and manifest through these churches His kingdom and His will *"on earth as it is in heaven"* (Matt. 6:10).

King David knew how to operate this key of Spirit-filled worship and praise; thus the prophetic realm of the glory of God was opened to him. He kept the doors of heaven open to his nation for his entire forty-year reign.

It is of paramount importance that churches in every nation learn to use this *"key of David"* as he did, so that the heavens can be opened and remain open, and the outpouring of Holy Spirit revival and revelation can occur on a worldwide scale. David's kingdom enjoyed the greatest period of victory in the history of Israel. He never lost a battle. He subdued all his enemies, and they all made peace with him. He passed on to Solomon, his son, an ordered, prosperous, and peaceful kingdom that became the high point of ruling and reigning in biblical history.

In the late 1940s, churches in Canada and the United States began to learn how to use this *"key of David,"* and a biblical practice of praise and worship began that released a tremendous wave of prophetic power and the glory of God for which the church had been longing for decades.

A generation later, churches that have been faithfully using this *"key of David"* are still moving in the prophetic anointing, are still enjoying the manifest presence of God expressed in the gifts and operations of the Holy Spirit, and are still basking in the glory of the Lord. Other assemblies across the world are putting these principles into operation and are enjoying the same outpouring of the Spirit of God, as the windows of heaven are being opened to them as well.

GOD INHABITS PRAISE

A fundamental Scripture that explains the *"key of David"* is Psalm 22:3: *"But thou art holy, O thou that inhabitest the praises of Israel"* (KJV). What a simple, yet profound, revelation! The King of Glory sits enthroned in the praises of His people. His presence as King is revealed to them in praise and worship. As His people worship Him, the revelatory ministry of the Holy Spirit is released, and the presence of God Himself becomes known. Believers have testified in worship to seeing the throne of God and experiencing a sense of being in the very courtroom of heaven at the feet of God Himself!

Biblical writers, describing similar experiences in their day, used words such as *appearance* or *likeness* to describe their visions of God and were limited to using earthly analogies, such as that the glory of God appeared like fire and light.

> *And above the firmament over their heads was the likeness of a throne, in appearance like a sapphire stone; on the likeness of the throne was a likeness with the appearance of a man high above it. Also from the appearance of His waist and upward I saw, as it were, the color of amber with the appearance of fire all around within it; and from the appearance of His waist and downward I saw, as it were, the appearance of fire with brightness all around. Like the appearance of a rainbow in a cloud on a rainy day, so was the appearance of the brightness all around it. This was the appearance of the likeness of the glory of the LORD.* (Ezek. 1:26–28)

His body was like beryl, his face like the appearance of lightning, his eyes like torches of fire, his arms and feet like burnished bronze in color, and the sound of his words like the voice of a multitude. (Dan. 10:6)

And in the midst of the seven lampstands [I saw] One like the Son of Man....His head and hair were white like wool, as white as snow, and His eyes like a flame of fire; His feet were like fine brass, as if refined in a furnace, and His voice as the sound of many waters. (Rev. 1:13–15)

What is exciting is that these same self-revelations of God are occurring again today—now—even as they did in biblical times. As the church stands worshiping her Lord, the curtain that normally hides the heavenly realm from earth is drawn back, and our spiritual eyes are opened to see the things of God: His awesome Person, truths of His Word, prophetic insight into the strategy of spiritual warfare, and His throne and His courtroom.

The apostle Paul describes this revelatory role of the Holy Spirit in our lives:

Eye has not seen, nor ear heard, nor have entered into the heart of man the things which God has prepared for those who love Him. But God has revealed them to us through His Spirit. (1 Cor. 2:9–10)

SPIRITUAL EYESIGHT

Such profound teaching! Things in the heavens that the natural *"eye has not seen,"* God has *"revealed them to us through His Spirit."* And He has chosen to do this in the worshiping congregation where He inhabits the praises of His people (Ps. 22:3). How can it be theologically correct to see things in the heavenly realm, when we are told in Scripture, *"For we walk by faith, not by sight"* (2 Cor. 5:7)? Is it really biblical then to see? Praise God, yes! We do not walk by natural sight, for we have never seen with our natural eyes the things of God in the heavens, for *"no one has seen God at any time"* (John 1:18). In fact, Jesus pronounced a greater blessing on those who never saw Him with their natural eyes, yet still believed: *"Thomas, because you have seen Me [naturally], you have believed. Blessed are those who have not seen and yet have believed"* (John 20:29).

Believers often look back with nostalgia to the distant past, longing to have been with the Lord as He walked the streets of Galilee, ministering to the multitudes. They wish they could have been in the upper room when the risen Christ appeared to His disciples. But Jesus said, *"Blessed are those who have not seen and yet have believed."*

Does this mean then that we are left to blindly cling to facts and doctrines of our faith with sheer mental determination, void of seeing or feeling anything? Thank God, no! There is a spiritual seeing and hearing with which we are endowed when we are born again. God is a Spirit. He sees and hears, and we receive His Spirit: *"He who planted the ear, shall He not hear? He who formed the eye, shall He not see?"* (Ps. 94:9).

We hear and see because He hears and sees. And when we are born again, God shares His abilities with us: *"Blessed are the pure in heart, for they shall see God"* (Matt. 5:8). *"Unless one is born again, he cannot see the kingdom of God"* (John 3:3).

God means for us to see, hear, and feel things concerning His kingdom—not with our natural faculties, but with new spiritual abilities. Faith has substance undergirding it; it is not blind: *"Now faith is the substance of things hoped for, the evidence of things not seen"* (Heb. 11:1). *"So then faith comes by hearing, and hearing by the word of God"* (Rom. 10:17).

EMOTIONAL FULFILLMENT

Once we have been born again by the Spirit, by believing on the Lord Jesus Christ, the Spirit of God brings to life in us spiritual sight, spiritual hearing, and even spiritual feelings and emotions.

There is an intellectualism in modern Christianity that is antagonistic to the possibility of any valid spiritual emotion, feeling, or vision. Such a reductionist mentality in the church has barred believers from a wonderfully biblical experience of God, to the great detriment of its followers.

Experiencing God's Power in Worship

We are meant to enjoy God and everything about God. We were created to find our greatest emotional and intellectual fulfillment in His presence. The first question of the *Westminster Shorter Catechism* answers a fundamental question:

"What is the chief end of man?"

"Man's chief end is to glorify God, and to enjoy Him for ever."

King David knew this, too. He wrote, *"In Your presence is fullness of joy; at Your right hand are pleasures forevermore"* (Ps. 16:11). *"There is a river whose streams shall make glad the city of God"* (Ps. 46:4).

Abundant Joy

The joy of the Lord is an actual anointing, an impartation by the Spirit of God to our lives that is unaffected by and independent of our natural circumstances. Jesus, the *"Man of sorrows and acquainted with grief"* (Isa. 53:3), was anointed by the Father with this spiritual joy beyond the capacity of anyone else in history.

"God...has anointed You with the oil of gladness more than Your companions" (Heb. 1:9). The Greek word here for gladness, *agalliao*, means "very much leaping" and signifies an abundant, overflowing joy that would cause one to leap and spring about, thus obviously touching and involving the emotions. At times in the early church, the disciples were *"filled with joy and with the Holy Spirit"* (Acts 13:52). Imagine being so filled with the joy of the Lord that in spite of your circumstances, with bleeding backs and chained bodies, you could sing praise to God at midnight, as Paul and Silas did, and bring down the house (Acts 16:25–26).

Jesus keeps His promises to put His joy in us and to make our joy full: *"These things I have spoken to you, that My joy may remain in you, and that your joy may be full"* (John 15:11). He gives us a double portion of joy. *His* joy is in us, and *our* joy is also full. As well as touching our emotions with His Spirit, God also opens our spiritual eyes to see what our natural eyes have not seen, and enables our spiritual ears to hear what our natural ears have not heard:

But as it is written: "Eye has not seen, nor ear heard, Nor have entered into the heart of man the things which God has prepared for those who love Him." But God has revealed them to us through His Spirit. For the Spirit searches all things, yes, the deep things of God.

(1 Cor. 2:9-10)

SEEING GOD

The apostle Paul prayed for the church that God would provide true spiritual vision and sight of the heavenly realm:

That the God of our Lord Jesus Christ, the Father of glory, may give to you the spirit of wisdom and revelation in the knowledge of Him, the eyes of your understanding being enlightened; that you may know what is the hope of His calling, what are the riches of the glory of His inheritance in the saints, and what is the exceeding greatness of His power toward us who believe. (Eph. 1:17–19)

Do you know that it is actually possible to spiritually see the God whom *"no one has* [naturally] *seen...at any time"* (John 1:18)? Isaiah saw Him:

In the year that King Uzziah died, I saw the Lord sitting on a throne, high and lifted up, and the train of His robe filled the temple. Above it stood seraphim; each one had six wings....And one cried to another and said: "Holy, holy, holy is the LORD of hosts; the whole earth is full of His glory!" (Isa. 6:1–3)

Job saw Him:

I have heard of You by the hearing of the ear, but now my eye sees You. Therefore I abhor myself, and repent in dust and ashes. (Job 42:5–6)

John saw Him:

Then I turned to see the voice that spoke with me. And having turned I saw seven golden lampstands, and in the midst of the seven lampstands One like the Son of Man....His eyes [were] like a flame of fire; His feet were like fine brass, as if refined in a furnace, and His voice as the sound of many waters...and His countenance was like the sun shining in its strength. And when I saw Him, I fell at His feet as dead. (Rev. 1:12–17)

Daniel saw Him:

I lifted my eyes and looked, and behold, a certain man clothed in linen....His face [was] like the appearance of lightning, his eyes like torches of fire, his arms and feet like burnished bronze in color, and the sound of his words like the voice of a multitude. And I, Daniel, alone saw the vision, for the men who were with me did not see the vision; but a great terror fell upon them, so that they fled to hide themselves. Therefore I was left alone when I saw this great vision, and no strength remained in me. (Dan. 10:5–8)

Ezekiel saw Him:

On the likeness of the throne was a likeness with the appearance of a man high above it. Also from the appearance of His waist and upward I saw, as it were, the color of amber with the appearance of fire all around within it; and from the appearance of His waist and downward I saw, as it were, the appearance of fire with brightness all around. (Ezek. 1:26–27)

Paul saw Him:

Am I not an apostle? Am I not free? Have I not seen Jesus Christ our Lord? (1 Cor. 9:1)

He rose again the third day according to the Scriptures....He was seen by James, then by all the apostles. Then last of all He was seen by me also, as one born out of due time. (1 Cor. 15:4, 7–8)

Does the Lord reveal Himself to us today, as He did in the days of the Bible? Are we simply to take these scriptural accounts by faith, believing that at least men in those days saw the Lord? Or can we pass through our faith in the written Word to an experience of actually seeing the Lord in the Spirit today? The glorious truth is that God is continuing to reveal Himself to our spiritual senses in times of worship and prayer, as He makes His presence known to us, and we see His glory.

GOD'S ABIDING PRESENCE

This opportunity of experiencing the presence of God is too little known by Christians today. They are doctrinally convinced of the omnipresence of God and also believe in His abiding presence in the life of the believer, but they are often ignorant of His *manifest* presence that can be experienced in worship, praise, prayer, and Bible study.

The omnipresence of God is a well-known Christian doctrine, by which we understand that the Spirit of God is everywhere present in His creation:

Where can I go from Your Spirit? Or where can I flee from Your presence? If I ascend into heaven, You are there; if I make my bed in hell, behold, You are there. If I take the wings of the morning, and dwell in the uttermost parts of the sea, even there Your hand shall lead me. (Ps. 139:7–10)

Each Christian should also be convinced of the abiding presence of God, by which we understand that God is permanently indwelling the life of every Christian, even when He is not perceived, felt, or experienced by the spiritual senses. Jesus said to those who are His: *"I will never leave you nor forsake you"* (Heb. 13:5).

But the most glorious aspect of the presence of God is His manifest presence, by which God reveals Himself to the spirit of the believer. This can occur in the private devotional life of the Christian at any time. It can also gloriously occur in Spirit-filled worship and praise, when the body of Christ comes together and begins to function supernaturally.

In the Psalms, we see a description of how the invisible God actually becomes visible through His body of worshipers. Just as a person's spirit is made visible by the movements of his body, the same is true of the Lord:

> *They have seen Your procession, O God, the procession of my God, my King, into the sanctuary.* [How did they see His *"procession"*? By the movements of His body, the church.] *The singers went before, the players on instruments followed after; among them were the maidens playing timbrels.*
>
> (Ps. 68:24–25)

The Spirit-motivated, worshiping congregation becomes the visible expression of the invisible God. This is what it means for the church to be the body of Christ—it is to visibly manifest what the Spirit is doing invisibly. The *New International Version* of the Bible translates Psalm 68:24: *"Your procession has come into view, O God."* Singers, instrumentalists, tambourines, and praise marches visibly demonstrate the movement, sight, and sound of God Himself.

Such fulfillment, such rapture at sensing the very presence and anointing of God Himself, can only be known by experience. The fact that the very God of heaven, the Creator of the heavens and the earth, humbles Himself to indwell and manifest His glory through the worshiping congregation is almost too wonderful to comprehend. Why would God do such a thing? Because in worship and praise, the heavenly atmosphere in which God eternally lives has been created here on earth; therefore, He can dwell here also!

In addition to being surrounded by worshiping hosts of angels in heaven, He is now surrounded here on earth by His own sons and daughters who are worshiping Him in spirit and in truth around His throne. In fact, He so desires communion with His people that when true worship occurs, He absolutely cannot resist coming! John told us that He is constantly searching the earth, actually seeking those who are worshiping Him in spirit and in truth. If we become true worshipers, rather than our having to frantically seek Him, He actually seeks us: *"For the Father is seeking such to worship Him"* (John 4:23).

When King David passed beyond the ritualism of the tabernacle of Moses and established his own tabernacle of worshipers in Zion, who sang praises to the Lord, shouted, clapped, danced, and bowed before the presence of the Lord, God could not restrain Himself any longer. He came down by His prophetic Spirit into the midst of the praising priesthood of Zion and declared: *"For the LORD has chosen Zion; He has desired it for His dwelling place: 'This is My resting place forever; here I will dwell, for I have desired it'"* (Ps. 132:13–14).

The same thing is happening in the present-day church. By becoming true worshipers, we prepare a habitation in which He can dwell. He comes and inhabits our praises and manifests His glory and presence to us. If only more churches knew this! Many well-meaning pastors and church leaders continually exhort their congregations, "Seek the Lord! Seek the Lord! Seek the Lord!" They don't seem to realize that if they would become true worshipers, God would seek them: *"But the hour is coming, and now is, when the true worshipers will worship the Father in spirit and truth; for the Father is seeking such to worship Him"* (John 4:23).

HE IS HERE

Here is the awesome truth about the consistent use of the *"key of David,"* which is Spirit-filled praise and worship. Any church, throughout its generations, can continue to experience not just an occasional visitation from God, but can actually become God's own dwelling place through praise and worship. Instead of sporadic visits in which God's presence is revealed to us, we can have Him permanently take up residence in our services, consistently manifesting Himself to us: *"For the LORD has chosen Zion; He has desired it for His dwelling place"* (Ps. 132:13).

We marvel at a God who would choose to disclose Himself to His creatures. What a privilege and awesome responsibility to experience the manifest presence of the Lord continually! It is more than just a take-it-by-faith assumption that in back of all our religious activity, God must be there, while never knowing, experiencing, or sensing Him. The same problem existed in the tabernacle of Moses during the days of David as they continued going through the motions of lighting candles, burning incense, setting forth bread, cleansing themselves in the water of purification, and offering animal sacrifices—acting as if God were there behind the scenes.

But in actual fact, He was not. During the days of David and his worshiping priesthood in Zion, the ark of the covenant, the place of the manifest presence of God, had been moved to the tabernacle of David. Behind the veil in the tabernacle of Moses, where the glory of God used to be, the Holy of Holies was now absolutely empty; it was a void, a black hole! Out in front of the curtain, acting as if God were still there, the priests and the Levites were faithfully carrying on their rituals and ceremonies.

Yet God was gone. He had transferred His manifest presence to the tabernacle of David in Zion, to a new kind of worship service. There, in the center of a praising priesthood, who sang, shouted, played their instruments, and danced for joy, was the ark of the covenant, the glory and presence of God:

> When God heard this, He was furious, and greatly abhorred Israel, so that He forsook the tabernacle of Shiloh [Moses' tabernacle], the tent He had [originally] placed among men....He...chose the tribe of Judah, Mount Zion [the tabernacle of David] which He loved.
>
> (Ps. 78:59–60, 67–68)

It was the same situation when David was anointed to be king. First Samuel 16:13 says, "The Spirit of the LORD came upon David from that day forward." The next verse says, "But the Spirit of the LORD departed from Saul" (v. 14). God could not equally bless David and Saul. He is progressive and moves His church forward into greater and greater liberty.

If God left Moses' tabernacle for David's, why do Christians today return to the ceremonialism and ritual of Moses' tabernacle, typified by burning candles and incense? Why don't they turn, instead, to the liberty, joy, and prophetic exuberance of the tabernacle of David? God abandoned the former to choose the latter. Shouldn't we? He sang through David's worshipers [we call it prophecy], played through them [we call it prophetic *music*], and moved through them [we call it *prophetic movement*].

Pastors, elders, worship leaders—the choice is yours. Will you have a church like Moses' or like David's? Both options are available today. There is a divine canopy of blessing that rests on every worshiping congregation that has discovered and is consistently using the *"key of David"*—worship of the Father *"in spirit* [prophetic anointing] *and truth* [according to the Scriptures]" (John 4:24).

> *Then the LORD will create above every dwelling place of Mount Zion, and above her assemblies, a cloud and smoke by day and the shining of a flaming fire by night. For over all the glory there will be a covering.* (Isa. 4:5)

Churches today that are consistently using the *"key of David"* never have a dry worship service. God is continually manifesting Himself to them through prophetic songs, through the revelation of His presence to the hearts of the worshipers, and through anointed music and inspired movement.

Chapter 11

Using the Key of David

How does such awesome, heaven-sent worship begin? Must we spend days in fasting and prayer? Is it only for mature Christians who have walked with God their whole lives? Do we need prominent preachers who can sway the masses? Is it necessary to artfully craft buildings that evoke religious responses? Must our church leaders be schooled in classes on liturgy? All the above may be helpful, but the real answer seems almost too easy. We enter such glorious worship through simple, childlike acts of obedience and praise.

HOW GOD WANTS TO BE WORSHIPED

Through songs inspired by the Holy Spirit, God patiently taught the priesthood in the tabernacle of David in Zion how He wanted to be worshiped. He sang through them prophetically in the Psalms and gave them His own worship instructions, or His own liturgy, concerning how they were to come before His presence:

Come before His presence with singing....Enter into His gates with thanksgiving, and into His courts with praise.
(Ps. 100:2, 4)

Behold, bless the LORD, all you servants of the LORD, who by night stand in the house of the LORD! Lift up your hands in the sanctuary, and bless the LORD! (Ps. 134:1–2)

Oh, clap your hands, all you peoples! Shout to God with the voice of triumph! (Ps. 47:1)

127

Experiencing God's Power in Worship

*Oh come, let us worship and bow down; let us kneel before
the LORD our Maker.* (Ps. 95:6)

Let them praise His name with the dance. (Ps. 149:3)

*Praise Him with the sound of the trumpet...with the lute
and harp! Praise Him with the timbrel and dance...with
stringed instruments and flutes! Praise Him...with clash-
ing cymbals!* (Ps. 150:3–5)

Behold the liturgy of the Psalms! It is a free-flowing blend
of expressive sound and movement through which God manifests Himself to His people. He delights in these simple acts of
faith and obedience to His instructions: singing, shouting, clapping, playing instruments, bowing, kneeling, and dancing. Even
children can participate in this glorious experience. Worship is
actually enjoyable! God intends for His worship services to be
joyful, life-giving, and energizing.

Although they are such simple acts of faith, a profound
work of God is accomplished in and through them, as the mani-
festation of His Holy presence changes us more and more into
His image. Isn't it just like God to conceal the deep revelation of
Himself in such simple acts of praise? While theologians and
Christian philosophers try to think their way into God, and
Christian religionists and liturgists try to work their way in
through humanly devised ceremonial acts, the God of Scripture
sits upon His throne in the heavens and cries out to us in the
Psalms, "Will you please try it My way?"

Acts of praise, such as singing with uplifted hands, clapping,
bowing, and dancing to the sounds of all manner of musical instruments, seem simple and innocent in themselves, yet in such
worship expressions, a dimension of the reality of the living God
unfolds that is truly astounding and life changing.

UPLIFTED HANDS

The lifting of hands in worship is a prime example of this
fact; there is such beauty and meaning expressed in this action.
Lifting our hands in worship to the Lord involves the opening of

our beings and our very hearts to Him: *"Let us lift our hearts and hands to God in heaven"* (Lam. 3:41).

God has intended such organic unity between body and soul that at the same time our hands are lifted to the Father in worship, our hearts are also to be lifted. The same Creator who gave us souls also gave us bodies with hands to beautifully express outwardly what our souls are experiencing inwardly in worship.

Worship expression must have therefore been intended by God in the original creation of our bodies. We have hands in order to be able to lift them to God in praise. We have mouths and voices to express worship verbally and musically to the Father. We have bodies to stand and to dance before Him in joy. We possess knees to physically express humility before our King, as we kneel in His presence.

The God of Creation formed our physical bodies for the purpose of visibly expressing to Him the worship of our invisible souls, so that the entire congregation of worshipers can coordinate and harmonize their worship together. We can all see and hear one another and be part of the corporate worship experience of God's people. The worship liturgies revealed by God in the Psalms were preordained in the very Creation itself. As we worship in simple obedience and faith, we win the victory over weakness and depression and open our souls and spirits to the Lord of glory.

The New Testament commands us to become strong and walk in victory through following this biblical liturgy of worship: *"Wherefore lift up the hands which hang down, and the feeble knees"* (Heb. 12:12 KJV).

We are to do this, as the context explains, even when we are being disciplined by God, so that our joy can be restored and we can walk in victory: *"And make straight paths for your feet, lest that which is lame be turned out of the way; but let it rather be healed"* (v. 13).

There is an incredible account of how Israel defeated the nation of Amalek simply because Moses kept his hands raised to the Lord:

And so it was, when Moses held up his hand, that Israel prevailed; and when he let down his hand, Amalek prevailed. But Moses' hands became heavy; so they took a stone and

Experiencing God's Power in Worship

put it under him, and he sat on it. And Aaron and Hur supported his hands, one on one side, and the other on the other side; and his hands were steady until the going down of the sun. (Exod. 17:11–12)

Some may spiritualize this passage and interpret the lifted hands of Moses as an example of the power of the intercession of church leaders, and, of course, this is true. The important fact here is that the physical act of the lifted hands visibly manifested the spiritual intercession and spiritual warfare in the heavenly realm, which actually affected the outcome of the battle and gave Israel the victory. Both body and soul were thus unified in the spirit of intercession.

Paul taught this same principle in the New Testament: *"I desire therefore that men pray everywhere, lifting up holy hands, without wrath and doubting"* (1 Tim. 2:8).

Why do Christian liturgists always seek to improve upon the simple commands of Scripture? After centuries of not worshiping with uplifted hands, it almost seems heretical to some to begin now. Yet in the beginning of the church, worship with uplifted hands was the normal practice. Why did the church ever stop worshiping this way, when both Old and New Testaments teach us to do so?

One answer can be found in a translation by Professor William Whiston of Cambridge University in 1737 of the *Antiquities of the Jews*, written by the Jewish historian Josephus in A.D. 93. Professor Whiston has his own revealing analysis of the beginning of Christian traditionalism, as he footnotes the comments of Josephus on the Old Testament passage where Moses stretched out his hand toward heaven, and the Amalekites were defeated:

This eminent circumstance, that while Moses's hands were lift up towards heaven, the Israelites prevailed ...seems to me the earliest intimation we have of the proper posture used of old in solemn prayer, which was the stretching out of the hands...towards heaven, as other passages of the Old and New Testament inform us. Nay, by the way, this posture seems to have continued in the Christian church, till the clergy, instead of learning their

130

prayers by heart, read them out of a book, which is in a great measure inconsistent with such an elevated posture, and which seems to me to have been only a later practice, introduced under the corrupt state of the church.

(Whiston 1974, 187)

The Bible teaches us that as we lift our hands in worship to the Father, a divine cycle of blessing is set in motion: *"Lift up your hands in the sanctuary, and bless the LORD. The LORD who made heaven and earth bless you from Zion!"* (Ps. 134:2–3).

As we bless Him with uplifted hands, He blesses us. And as we are blessed by Him, we have even more reason to return the blessing to Him in worship, which then produces more blessing for us; and soon, a mighty cycle of Holy Spirit blessing is set in motion, flowing up and back, up and back, from us to God and back from God to us again.

BLESS THE LORD

The congregation initiates this process by obeying Psalm 134:2. We are commanded to bless Him first; then He blesses us. What a wonderful revelation! We don't have to wait for any special anointing, feeling, or unction from God. We are not dependent on the right atmosphere or leading of the Holy Spirit. God simply teaches us, "Stand in the sanctuary, lift up your hands, begin blessing Me, and I will do the rest."

If worship leaders and pastors only understood this principle! Using the *"key of David"* (Rev. 3:7) is our responsibility. It is our glorious privilege. Think of it! We can stand under the outpoured blessing of the One who created the heavens and the earth and experience that blessing simply by beginning to lift up our hands and bless the Lord. No wonder David used this key often. Even in the wilderness of Judah when he fled from Saul and was being hunted down as a criminal by the armies of Israel, he used this key of worship: *"Because Your lovingkindness is better than life, my lips shall praise You. Thus I will bless You while I live; I will lift up my hands in Your name"* (Ps. 63:3–4).

Experiencing God's Power in Worship

Worshiping the Lord with extended hands is also revealed in the linguistic meaning of the Hebrew verb for praise, *yadah*, which means "to revere or worship with extended hands" and comes from the root word *yad*, simply meaning the "open hand."

CLAP YOUR HANDS

Other liturgies of worship, such as the clapping of hands, are found in Scripture and are now being practiced in the present-day church. Is it too hard to imagine that a universally accepted form of acclaim and approval in many cultures, a spontaneous show of joy by children at Christmas time, and an expression of appreciation at concerts and sporting events could also apply to God? Why not also applaud Him? Obviously, the value of His presence far exceeds any earthly joy. Why not freely express this form of appreciation in worship? *"Oh, clap your hands, all you peoples! Shout to God with the voice of triumph!"* (Ps. 47:1).

The prophet Isaiah even saw trees in the field clapping their hands with the joy of the Lord, later interpreting that we ourselves are these trees.

> *For you shall go out with joy, and be led out with peace; the mountains and the hills shall break forth into singing before you, and all the trees of the field shall clap their hands.* (Isa. 55:12)

> *To console those who mourn in Zion, to give them beauty for ashes, the oil of joy for mourning, the garment of praise for the spirit of heaviness; that they may be called trees of righteousness, the planting of the LORD.* (Isa. 61:3)

The psalmist cried out, *"Let the sea roar, and all its fullness, the world and those who dwell in it; let the rivers clap their hands; let the hills be joyful together before the LORD"* (Ps. 98:7–9).

Let the sea of humanity rejoice before the Lord! We clap for our heavenly King as Israel did for its earthly ones: *"They made him king and anointed him, and they clapped their hands and said, 'Long live the king!'"* (2 Kings 11:12).

So rejoice in your services of worship and *"clap your hands, all you peoples! Shout to God with the voice of triumph!"* (Ps. 47:1). Ah, the *"voice of triumph!"* It is a primordial, exuberant victory shout in the Holy Spirit.

Shout in Praise to God

There are times in biblical worship when the power of God is so strongly sensed in our hearts that the only appropriate response is to shout with all our might. It is not surprising to find throughout Scripture the release of a great volume of noise and shouts, as the power of the Spirit was released in the people of God. The very power of the sound of the shout of praise itself is therefore an expression of the power of God.

Shout joyfully to the LORD, all the earth; break forth in song, rejoice, and sing praises. Sing to the LORD with the harp, with the harp and the sound of a psalm, with trumpets and the sound of a horn; shout joyfully before the LORD, the King. (Ps. 98:4–6)

Sing to Him a new song; play skillfully with a shout of joy. (Ps. 33:3)

And Jehoshaphat bowed his head with his face to the ground, and all Judah and the inhabitants of Jerusalem bowed before the LORD, worshiping the LORD. Then the Levites...stood up to praise the LORD God of Israel with voices loud and high. (2 Chron. 20:18–19)

The whole multitude of the disciples began to rejoice and praise God with a loud voice for all the mighty works they had seen....Some of the Pharisees called to Him from the crowd, "Teacher, rebuke your disciples." But He answered and said to them, "I tell you that if these should keep silent, the stones would immediately cry out." (Luke 19:37, 39–40)

Was Jesus exaggerating here or taking poetic license? Was it really true that if the surge of praise from the disciples were shut off that shouts of acclamation would actually explode from the rocks in the fields around them? Apparently.

Look at other examples from Scripture of the intense volume of praise. Elizabeth was filled with the Holy Spirit, and *"she spoke out with a loud voice"* (Luke 1:42). *"And all the people went up after him; and the people played the flutes and rejoiced with great joy, so that the earth seemed to split with their sound"* (1 Kings 1:40).

Has the earth split open by the volume of the praise in our congregations recently?

> *The priests stood in their apparel with trumpets, and the Levites...with cymbals, to praise the LORD....And they sang responsively, praising and giving thanks to the LORD. ...Then all the people shouted with a great shout....But many of the priests...wept with a loud voice when the foundation of this temple was laid before their eyes. Yet many shouted aloud for joy, so that the people could not discern the noise of the shout of joy from the noise of the weeping of the people, for the people shouted with a loud shout, and the sound was heard afar off.* (Ezra 3:10–13)

> *The singers sang loudly....Also that day they offered great sacrifices, and rejoiced, for God had made them rejoice with great joy; the women and the children also rejoiced, so that the joy of Jerusalem was heard afar off.* (Neh. 12:42–43)

> *Then they took an oath before the LORD with a loud voice, with shouting and trumpets and rams' horns. And all Judah rejoiced at the oath, for they had sworn with all their heart and sought Him with all their soul; and He was found by them.* (2 Chron. 15:14–15)

What a beautiful picture of praise! The people were loving God with all their strength, putting all their hearts and souls into their worship of Him, investing all their desire in the Lord Himself, and it was reflected in the sheer volume and noise of their worship—again the physical sound of praise mirroring and expressing the spiritual intensity within them.

"He was found by them." The presence of God was actually discovered, encountered, and experienced. Could it be that He is never really *"found"* by many present-day churches because of their lethargic, lukewarm attempts at worship? *"And you will seek Me and find Me, when you search for Me with all your heart. I will be found by you, says the LORD"* (Jer. 29:13–14).

One reason for the shout of triumph in worship is that our spirits are attuned to the Spirit of God that rules in the heavenly realm. Our victory shouts express on earth what is happening in the heavens, as in Jehoshaphat's mighty military victory: *"Now when they began to sing and to praise, the LORD set ambushes against the people of Ammon, Moab, and Mount Seir, who had come against Judah; and they were defeated"* (2 Chron. 20:22).

Look at this example from the days of King Abijah:

And when Judah looked around, to their surprise the battle line was at both front and rear; and they cried out to the LORD, and the priests sounded the trumpets. Then the men of Judah gave a shout; and as the men of Judah shouted, it happened that God struck Jeroboam and all Israel before Abijah and Judah. (2 Chron. 13:14–16)

This connection between the shout of victory and the defeat of the enemy is most well-known in the battle of Jericho:

Joshua said to the people: "Shout, for the LORD has given you the city!"...So the people shouted when the priests blew the trumpets. And it happened when the people heard the sound of the trumpet, and the people shouted with a great shout, that the wall fell down flat....And they took the city. (Josh. 6:16, 20)

Shouting and clapping for joy, lifting hands, and pouring out one's heart in worship to the Father are the liturgies of the Psalms—physical expressions of what the soul and spirit are doing in worship, as body and soul are unified in expressing the divine emotions of the Spirit.

135

Experiencing God's Power in Worship

BOW DOWN BEFORE GOD

None of the expressions of worship found in Scripture is as awesome as bowing, kneeling, or prostrating oneself before the Lord. The Hebrew word for glory, *kabod,* is one of the most wonderful words in the Bible. It means "weight" or to "be heavy." The apostle Paul in 2 Corinthians 4:17 talked about the *"eternal weight of glory"* that we are to experience. This can become a reality in worship. Sometimes the presence of God is actually sensed by the worshiper as a pressure upon his spirit, a weightiness that is felt to rest on him. In biblical language, the Holy Spirit is described as coming or even falling upon people:

> *They sent Peter and John to them, who, when they had come down, prayed for them that they might receive the Holy Spirit. For as yet He had fallen upon none of them. They had only been baptized in the name of the Lord Jesus.*
> (Acts 8:14–16)

"While Peter was still speaking these words, the Holy Spirit fell upon all those who heard the word" (Acts 10:44).

Sometimes the presence of God is perceived to be resting so heavily upon the worshipers that the only proper response is to bow, kneel, or even prostrate oneself before the King of Glory.

> *When they lifted up their voice with the trumpets and cymbals and instruments of music, and praised the LORD...the house, the house of the LORD, was filled with a cloud, so that the priests could not continue ministering because of the cloud; for the glory [or weight] of the LORD filled the house of God.* (2 Chron. 5:13–14)

> *When all the children of Israel saw how the fire came down, and the glory [or heaviness] of the LORD on the temple, they bowed their faces to the ground on the pavement, and worshiped and praised the LORD.* (2 Chron. 7:3)

Psalm 95 urges us to acknowledge the majesty of our great God and King by humbling ourselves before Him as His loyal subjects: *"Oh come, let us worship and bow down; let us kneel before the LORD our Maker"* (v. 6).

136

Encounters with the Being of the Lord have sometimes caused people to actually fall at His feet and to lose all their strength in the presence of His mighty person:

> *And I, Daniel, alone saw the vision, for the men who were with me did not see the vision; but a great terror fell upon them, so that they fled to hide themselves. Therefore I was left alone when I saw this great vision, and no strength remained in me....Yet I heard the sound of his words; and while I heard the sound of his words I was in a deep sleep on my face, with my face to the ground. Suddenly, a hand touched me, which made me tremble on my knees and on the palms of my hands. And he said to me, "O Daniel, man greatly beloved, understand the words that I speak to you, and stand upright."...While he was speaking this word to me, I stood trembling.* (Dan. 10:7–11)

In the glory of heaven itself, the presence of the Lord is so awe inspiring and so wonderful, that the worshipers are often overcome by it. The twenty-four elders have seats provided for them, but they are usually seen falling before the Lamb in worship:

> *Now when He had taken the scroll, the four living creatures and the twenty-four elders fell down before the Lamb, each having a harp, and golden bowls full of incense, which are the prayers of the saints.* (Rev. 5:8)

> *Then the four living creatures said, "Amen!" And the twenty-four elders fell down and worshiped Him who lives forever and ever.* (v. 14)

> *And the twenty-four elders who sat before God on their thrones fell on their faces and worshiped God.* (Rev. 11:16)

> *All the angels stood around the throne and the elders and the four living creatures, and fell on their faces before the throne and worshiped God.* (Rev. 7:11)

The apostle John was overcome with the presence of the Lord: *"And when I saw Him, I fell at His feet as dead. But He laid His right hand on me, saying to me, 'Do not be afraid; I am the First and the Last'"* (Rev. 1:17).

The physical body of the worshiper actually manifests what his spirit is experiencing, bowing low under the heaviness, weight, and glory of the presence of the Lord.

Chapter 12

Praise Him in the Dance

*B*ecause God loves to manifest His Word in actions visible to our natural eyes, it comes as no surprise to discover that God loves our joy in His presence to be manifested in actual physical expressions of rejoicing in all forms of the dance.

If the body exists to show visibly what the Spirit is doing invisibly, and if the powerful joy of the Lord is to be experienced in our lives, then it is reasonable to find in the Word of God occasions when the Holy Spirit motivated God's people to express this joy of the Lord in various forms of dancing and rejoicing. These expressions range from leaping and skipping for joy to twisting and twirling with all one's might, and from rejoicing and celebrating in circle dances and festival praise processions to bowing and kneeling before the Lord.

Everything is there in the original languages of Scripture. The variety of forms of movement hidden in the biblical Hebrew and Greek words for dance have largely remained undiscovered throughout the centuries of both Catholic and Protestant church traditions, which have categorically ruled out dancing in worship to God. Jesus' declaration to the Pharisees, *"You nullify the word of God for the sake of your tradition"* (Matt. 15:6 NIV) applies nowhere more clearly than in the church's lack of understanding of the wealth of biblical teaching on the physical expressions of dances, marches, and processions in worship and in its refusal to praise the Lord *"with tambourine and dancing"* (Ps. 150:4 NIV).

Although the church has historically refused to rejoice in the dance, the secular world certainly has not. Most cultures of the earth express their joy in all forms of ritualistic dancing. In the rebellious countercultures of the Western world, the dance has been widely used to promote and express sensuality, lust, promiscuity, and other forms of rebellion. The Christian church looks at such a prostitution of the dance and cries, "We were right! Look how evil it is!" and reacts even more strongly against physical movement in worship services.

JOY IN THE DANCE

But just as music itself and the use of instruments and song can be expressed in either worship to God or in the service of evil, so it is with the dance. In spite of its perversion in the world, it can definitely have a holy and sacred purpose. Many churches are now returning to this ancient biblical form of worship to discover that not only is there tremendous joy released in praising God in the dance, but also an associated liberty of the Holy Spirit is produced, which releases a greater freedom for all kinds of prophetic activity that goes far beyond the dance itself. By prohibiting the use of dance in the church, we have been denying the divine Artist the use of a brilliant color for painting His worship canvas. By releasing the dance in worship, we allow the Lord to add this beautiful hue to His worship palette. By freeing our bodies to worship the Lord in the dance, we are also setting free the Holy Spirit, not only to express His joy in us in physical movement, but also to manifest the physical demonstrations of prophecy that so often occurred in biblical times when people acted out spiritual concepts in visible ways. Joy is meant by God to be expressed just as visibly as prophecy is.

THE PRAISE PARADE

The eternal, unseen God wants to become visibly active in our worship services today, moving and flowing with grace and power through His body on earth. In fact, the only way God can become visible in this world is through His body. *"No one has seen God at any time"* (1 John 4:12), we are told, and yet Psalm 68 declares, *"They have seen Your procession, O God, the procession of my God, my King, into the sanctuary"* (v. 24).

How can this be? How can the invisible God be seen going into His sanctuary? Because God, who is spirit, has a body, His church, and the function of that body is to visibly manifest the intentions, thoughts, and will of the invisible Person who inhabits it. When the invisible Spirit of God energizes and motivates His body, the church, to express joyful exuberance and prophetic action in *"the sanctuary,"* then His *"goings"* (v. 24 KJV) become visible.

The Hebrew word for *"goings"* is *haliykah* and means "a walking" and by implication "a procession, march, or caravan." The NIV translation says simply, *"Your procession has come into view, O God"* (v. 24). Think of it. It is *"Your procession...O God."* It is His parade; He is marching. The unseen God is moving in the sanctuary when His body moves. King David described this praise parade as all the tribes marched in praise processions before the Lord:

> *In front are the singers, after them the musicians; with them are the maidens playing tambourines....There is the little tribe of Benjamin, leading them, there the great throng of Judah's princes, and there the princes of Zebulun and of Naphtali.* (Ps. 68:25, 27 NIV)

When God is on the move, His people are on the move, as heaven and earth unite in one grand, concerted effort. The unseen God moves through His visible body in actions of praise and worship that can be seen and experienced. Psalm 68 portrays Israel's march through the wilderness as linked to the moving of God in the heavenly realm that was above them, the unseen God moving *"on high"* (Ps. 92:8), as His people, His visible manifestation, marched on the earth:

> *Sing to God, sing praise to his name, extol him who rides on the clouds—his name is the LORD—and rejoice before him....When you went out before your people, O God, when you marched through the wasteland,* Selah *the earth shook, the heavens poured down rain, before God.* (Ps. 68:4, 7–8 NIV)

King David experienced exactly the same unity between the movement of God in the heavens and the movement of his own army on earth. He was directed to attack the Philistines when he heard *"the sound of marching in the tops of the balsam* [mulberry] *trees...because that will mean God has gone out in front of* [him] *to strike the Philistine army"* (1 Chron. 14:15 NIV). As God moved invisibly to help him defeat his enemies, David marched out visibly to attack his foes. Not surprisingly, he won a great victory.

DANCE FOR JOY

God became visible. He manifested Himself on earth through His body. What a powerful experience! When the joy of the Lord is released within us, it is impossible to passively and unemotionally manage and control it. We are talking about the powerful joy of our Creator being poured into our finite beings. When this happened in Scripture and as it is happening again today, shouts of joy ring out. People twist, spin, and twirl, leap, jump, and skip with all their might.

King David could hardly contain himself. The presence of God was returning to Jerusalem! Everything was ready. A new tabernacle had been erected on Mount Zion, and the singers and musicians were ready. The glorious ark of the covenant was moving up the road toward Zion. The joy of the Lord filled the king and the people to overflowing. The day David had been waiting for had arrived:

> *So all Israel brought up the ark of the covenant of the LORD with shouts, with the sounding of rams' horns and trumpets, and of cymbals, and the playing of lyres and harps.* (1 Chron. 15:28 NIV)

> *David, wearing a linen ephod, danced* [in Hebrew, whirled] *before the LORD with all his might, while he and the entire house of Israel brought up the ark of the LORD with shouts and the sound of trumpets. As the ark of the LORD was entering the City of David, Michal daughter of Saul watched from a window. And...she saw King David leaping and dancing before the LORD.* (2 Sam. 6:14–16 NIV)

What caused David to twist and twirl before the Lord with all his might? The experience of his joy! The Scripture teaches us that there is an actual anointing, an *"oil of gladness"* (Ps. 45:7), that is available to us, and Jesus experienced this joy more than anyone else:

> *But to the Son He says:...* *"You have loved righteousness and hated lawlessness; therefore God, Your God, has anointed You with the oil of gladness more than Your companions."*   (Heb. 1:8–9)

What is this *"oil of joy"* (v. 9 NIV) that Jesus has received more than anyone else? The Greek word for it is *agalliasis,* which is compounded from *agan,* meaning "much," and *liao,* meaning "jumping or leaping." This word literally means to "leap very much for joy," to "be exceeding glad," to "rejoice greatly," to receive a joy so strong that it causes one to spring about and jump for joy. Jesus was anointed with such a joy, a Holy Spirit-filled joy and gladness, the kind of joy He will feel when He returns for His bride, to celebrate with her in His wedding dances: *"The voice of my beloved! Behold, he comes leaping upon the mountains, skipping upon the hills"* (Song 2:8).

Jesus shares this leaping, skipping, bubbling joy with us. He said to His disciples, *"These things I have spoken to you, that My joy may remain in you, and that your joy may be full"* (John 15:11). This joy is a glorious double portion. We can have His powerful joy in us, and our own joy becomes full as well. No wonder we shout and dance! The same joy that caused David to twirl before God with all his might is the same joy that will cause our Bridegroom to return for His bride, leaping upon the mountains and skipping upon the hills. Is it any wonder that this joy is expressed physically?

TOO MUCH JOY?

Such abandonment in worship is awesome and beautiful to behold. And yet, for some, it is too much—too much love, too much worship, too much joy. Like Michal, David's wife, some are offended by anyone who loves God's presence more than they do and cannot help judging those who abandon themselves in joyful worship:

> *Now as the ark of the LORD came into the City of David,*
> *Michal, Saul's daughter, looked through a window and*
> *saw King David leaping and whirling before the LORD;*
> *and she despised him in her heart.* (2 Sam. 6:16)

When he got home, she rebuked him, and he was forced to defend his own abandonment in worship:

> *It was before the LORD...I will celebrate before the LORD. I*
> *will become even more undignified than this, and I will be*
> *humiliated in my own eyes. But...I will be held in honor.*
> (vv. 21–22 NIV)

What did God think of Michal's judgmental attack on her worshiping husband? *"Therefore Michal the daughter of Saul had no children to the day of her death"* (v. 23). Her barrenness of spirit brought a barrenness to her whole life.

God loves those who love Him with all their hearts, souls, minds, and strength. When we love Him this way, we fulfill His greatest commandment:

> *Then one of the scribes came, and...asked Him, "Which is*
> *the first commandment of all?" Jesus answered him, "The*
> *first of all the commandments is...'You shall love the LORD*
> *your God with all your heart, with all your soul, with all*
> *your mind, and with all your strength.'"* (Mark 12:28–30)

God loved David, or rather was able to love David so much, because David loved Him with everything he had.

DIFFERENT FORMS OF WORSHIP

Throughout the history of the Old Testament, men and women have exulted in the Lord with great joy, which was often expressed in various forms of dancing. The full range of these dance expressions has not been understood in our culture because our English translations of the Bible do not accurately convey the variety of dance forms found in the original biblical languages. The generic word *dance* is used to cover them all. It would be like using the word *food* to translate words describing very different kinds of diet.

Question: What did the Israelites eat in the wilderness?

Answer: Food. (But what kind?)

Question: How did the Israelites rejoice before God?

Answer: In the dance. (But what kind?)

Following the overthrow of the Egyptian army in the Red Sea, the prophetess Miriam took her tambourine and led the women of Israel in victory dances on the eastern shore of the sea, as they celebrated the power of Jehovah in *mecholah*— circles of female dancers, spinning and twirling for joy in the presence of the Lord of Hosts. (See Exodus 15:20.)

In the annual festival of the Lord in Shiloh, the women of Israel were rejoicing in the Hebrew dance form *chul* or *chil*, meaning "to spin around, to go in a circle." (See Judges 21:21.)

The joyful dancing of King David is described in different accounts by several Hebrew words: *karar*—"to dance, whirl, or move in a circle" (2 Sam. 6:14), *reqad*—"to spring about wildly, dance, jump, leap, or skip" (1 Chron. 15:29), and *pazaz*—"to leap, bound, to be light or agile" (2 Sam. 6:16).

The Bridegroom returns, as seen prophetically by His lover (the church), expressing His joy in the dance form *dalag,* as He rejoices by leaping and skipping upon the mountains: *"The voice of my beloved! Behold, he comes leaping upon the mountains, skipping upon the hills"* (Song 2:8).

The prophetic Spirit came upon the psalmists in David's day and taught them how God wanted to be praised: *"Praise Him with the timbrel and dance"* (Ps. 150:4). *"Let them praise His name with the dance"* (Ps. 149:3).

The Hebrew word for dance in these worship instructions in Psalms 149 and 150 is *machowl,* "a round dance," from *chul* or *chil,* meaning to "twist and twirl around." Israel historically has been known to be a people who know well how to rejoice in the dance. Even to this day, Jewish cultural dance forms are very well-known.

In its ancient history, God called Israel to Jerusalem three times a year just to fellowship together and to rejoice before Him with great joy in their feast days. The Hebrew word for feast has as its root meaning the word *chagag*, which means "to move in a circle, specifically to march in a sacred procession, to observe a festival, to celebrate, to keep a solemn feast, by implication to be giddy or drunken."

Even in their prophetic glimpses into the future, the prophets of Israel envisioned the people of God rejoicing in the Day of the Lord with great joy and dancing:

Again I will build you, and you shall be rebuilt, O virgin of Israel! You shall again be adorned with your tambourines, and shall go forth in the dances of those who rejoice....Then shall the virgin rejoice in the dance, and the young men and the old, together; for I will turn their mourning to joy, will comfort them, and make them rejoice rather than sorrow. (Jer. 31:4, 13)

This joy foreseen by the prophets began to break forth in the early church as the last days began on the Day of Pentecost. As the Holy Spirit fell upon the disciples, evidenced by visible tongues of fire, they acted like they were intoxicated with new wine. Peter had to defend how they were acting: *"These men are not drunk, as you suppose. It's only nine in the morning!"* (Acts 2:15 NIV).

The joy of the Lord coming upon people caused leaping and dancing on other occasions in the New Testament. When Mary arrived at the home of Zacharias to share with Elizabeth the angelic visitation she had received, Elizabeth was filled with the Holy Spirit and began to prophesy with a loud voice. Simultaneously, the Holy Spirit also filled the unborn son in her womb, and little John the Baptist, three months before his birth, began to leap and dance for joy:

When Elizabeth heard the greeting of Mary,...the babe leaped in her womb; and Elizabeth was filled with the

146

Holy Spirit. Then she spoke out with a loud voice and said, "Blessed are you among women, and blessed is the fruit of your womb!...As soon as the voice of your greeting sounded in my ears, the babe leaped in my womb for joy."
(Luke 1:41–42, 44)

Zacharias, the father of John the Baptist, had been told by the angel that his son would be *"filled with the Holy Spirit, even from his mother's womb"* (v. 15). And when Mary's greeting reached Elizabeth's ears, it happened. The Holy Spirit filled his mother and the unborn son simultaneously, and little John began to leap and dance for joy as his mother began to prophesy.

The Scripture says he *"leaped...for joy"* (v. 44)—the same kind of joy that would one day anoint his cousin, Jesus—*agalliasis,* to "jump, leap, spring up for joy." We are told that this same kind of joy became an anointing oil, which was placed upon Jesus to a degree that no one else has ever experienced (Heb. 1:9). This kind of joy is found often in the New Testament. We are to rejoice this way when we are persecuted because of our righteousness (Matt. 5:12). The parallel passage in Luke uses another Greek verb, *skirtao,* which means the same thing: *"Rejoice in that day and leap for joy! For indeed your reward is great in heaven"* (Luke 6:23).

JOYFUL WEDDING DANCES

Agalliasis, "very much leaping," is also to be the joy of the last days; it is most often associated in the New Testament with the future return of the Lord Jesus Christ:

But rejoice to the extent that you partake of Christ's sufferings, that when His glory is revealed, you may also be glad with exceeding joy. (1 Pet. 4:13)

Now to Him who is able to keep you from stumbling, and to present you faultless before the presence of His glory with exceeding joy. (Jude 24)

Let us be glad and rejoice and give Him glory, for the marriage of the Lamb has come. (Rev. 19:7)

Experiencing God's Power in Worship

The wedding dances of the Lamb of God occur as He returns for His bride, *"leaping upon the mountains, skipping upon the hills"* (Song 2:8). What a glorious prospect for our future! Is it nearer than we think? These last days began with the outpoured Holy Spirit on the Day of Pentecost almost two thousand years ago, but that was only two days ago in God's time frame, for *"one day is as a thousand years, and a thousand years as one day"* (2 Pet. 3:8). Are these last days coming to their culmination and fulfillment in a glorious reunion of the Bridegroom and His bride? Is this why the wedding dances of joy are breaking out in the church of Jesus Christ today across the whole world? Is this why the church in this generation is rediscovering the worship liturgy of the tabernacle of David, with its joyful expressions of worship, as the liberty and joy of the people of God are expressed in shouting, leaping, dancing, clapping, bowing, kneeling, prostrating, marching, and processing with joyful songs of praise and worship?

Did the prophet Amos foresee our day, when he prophesied twenty-seven hundred years ago: *"On that day I will raise up the tabernacle of David, which has fallen down, and repair its damages; I will raise up its ruins, and rebuild it as in the days of old"* (Amos 9:11)?

We know that the apostle James, as the last days began, quoted this prophecy and applied it to the early church, as he explained why the Gentiles were being drawn to the Lord:

> *And after they had become silent, James answered, saying, "Men and brethren, listen to me: Simon has declared how God at the first visited the Gentiles to take out of them a people for His name. And with this the words of the prophets agree, just as it is written: 'After this I will return and will rebuild the tabernacle of David, which has fallen down; I will rebuild its ruins, and I will set it up; so that the rest of mankind may seek the LORD, even all the Gentiles who are called by My name, says the LORD who does all these things.'"* (Acts 15:13–17)

Now, "two days" later, at the close of the second millennium of church history, God is again restoring to the church the joy, liberty, and worship expressions originally born in the tabernacle

148

of David. This great joy in the presence of the Lord is again being expressed in all the physical forms of the dance, as in David's day. It is a foretaste of the *"fullness of joy"* (Ps. 16:11), which is awaiting us in the coming fullness of the kingdom of God: *"After two days* [two thousand years?] *He will revive us; on the third day He will raise us up, that we may live in His sight"* (Hos. 6:2).

O church of Jesus Christ! Listen to the worship liturgies of the Psalms. Cease from your own traditions that nullify the Word of God; instead, follow the ancient tradition that brings life to the church and releases the prophetic Spirit of God:

Praise Him with the timbrel and dance. (Ps. 150:4)

Let them praise His name with the dance. (Ps. 149:3)

You turned my wailing into dancing. (Ps. 30:11 NIV)

Certainly the church of Jesus Christ has the scriptural right to rejoice in these ways! If we are taught by the apostle Paul to worship the Lord with *"psalms and hymns and spiritual songs"* (Eph. 5:19), then surely we can go to these same Psalms for our worship instructions.

Jesus was not embarrassed about dancing. His view of His Father's house (the church) included this expression of joyful worship. When the Prodigal Son returned, Jesus said, the household began to celebrate. Meanwhile the older son was in the field. When he came near the house, he heard *"music and dancing"* (Luke 15:25). The Jewish culture was certainly not embarrassed by dancing. When the lame man was healed by Peter and John, he entered into the temple area, *"walking, leaping, and praising God"* (Acts 3:8). And no usher came over and said, "Not here, sir."

Jesus leaped and rejoiced in the Spirit. *"At that time Jesus, full of joy* [agalliasis—very much leaping] *through the Holy Spirit, said, 'I praise you, Father'"* (Luke 10:21 NIV).

He was rejoicing *"through the Holy Spirit."* So should we today! His body, filled with His anointing *"oil of joy"* (Heb. 1:9 NIV), is today rejoicing with *"joy unspeakable and full of glory"*

Experiencing God's Power in Worship

(1 Pet. 1:8 KJV). We are manifesting in our worship services with our physical bodies what the Spirit of the Lord is doing within us. He is energizing His body on earth to manifest and display the glory and beauty of His eternal joy, by moving His church to visibly express this joy in dances, marches, praise processions, and prophetic movement.

Chapter 13

Victory Marches

We have seen how the movement of the people of God on earth can be linked with the moving of God's mighty Spirit in the heavenlies. When Israel marched through the wilderness, it was God marching, too.

When you went out before your people, O God, when you marched through the wasteland, Selah *the earth shook, the heavens poured down rain, before God.* (Ps. 68:7 NIV)

The power of God was often released on earth as the people of God marched in obedience to His Word. When Israel passed through the Red Sea, Egypt was destroyed behind them. When they marched through the wilderness on their way to the Land of Promise, the presence of God was with them so powerfully that their enemies could not curse them. Balaam learned this as he looked down that day from Mount Nebo, where he had been taken by the king of Moab to bring a curse upon Israel:

How shall I curse whom God has not cursed?...The LORD *his God is with him, and the shout of a King is among them....There is no sorcery against Jacob, nor any divination against Israel.* (Num. 23:8, 21, 23)

Later in their wilderness journey, when it came time for Israel to march around Jericho for seven days, the power of God slowly built up enough force around them to level the city with a giant earthquake. This just happened to coincide with their victory shout, and the walls of the city fell down flat:

Experiencing God's Power in Worship

> *So the people shouted when the priests blew the trumpets....And the people shouted with a great shout, that the wall fell down flat. Then the people went up into the city...and they took the city.* (Josh. 6:20)

At the end of the history of the Old Testament, when Israel had finished rebuilding the walls of Jerusalem after their return from Babylon, they appointed two groups of worshipers to march in opposite directions upon the wall of the city, encircling Jerusalem with their praise and thanksgiving to God for giving them the victory:

> *So I brought the leaders of Judah up on the wall, and appointed two large thanksgiving choirs. One went to the right hand on the wall....The other thanksgiving choir went the opposite way.* (Neh. 12:31, 38)

When Jesus entered Jerusalem as its coming King, He rode in a sacred procession, as His disciples shouted in praise and acclamation, casting their garments on the road and waving palm branches in worship (Matt. 21:8–9).

> *And as He went, many spread their clothes on the road. Then, as He was now drawing near the descent of the Mount of Olives, the whole multitude of the disciples began to rejoice and praise God with a loud voice...saying: "Blessed is the King who comes in the name of the LORD!"* (Luke 19:36–38)

The power of God moving in the heavenly realm was so great that it set all the authorities of the city into an uproar, and they frantically began scurrying about, planning how they would destroy Him.

THE EFFECT OF PRAISE MARCHES

Praise processions, then, can have a great spiritual impact upon a city, a region, or a nation. Marches and gatherings of Christians in seats of government and in nations' capitals continue to have great effect in spiritual warfare to this day and are being widely practiced by the church. We can also celebrate victories achieved and help to maintain them by displaying to the onlooking world the fact of our enemies' defeat. In Jehoshaphat's day, after God had sent ambushments against the enemies of Israel and they had destroyed themselves, Israel celebrated its victory with a triumphant march back to Jerusalem with King Jehoshaphat leading the parade:

> *Then they returned, every man of Judah and Jerusalem, with Jehoshaphat in front of them, to go back to Jerusalem with joy, for the LORD had made them rejoice over their enemies. So they came to Jerusalem, with stringed instruments and harps and trumpets, to the house of the LORD.*
> (2 Chron. 20:27–28)

Rev. Steve Griffing, in an insightful analysis of this passage in *The Worship of the Psalms in the Twentieth-century Church*, points out the relationship between Jehoshaphat's spiritual warfare and the celebration march that followed:

> [Second Chronicles 20:27–28] describes the delirious joy and great pageantry with which they celebrated God's victory. This is as much a part of the battle plan as the actual confrontation; for in pageantry and celebration they published God's goodness to the nation and memorialized the goings of God to the next generation.
>
> This type of free celebration is not emphasized enough in our churches as a means of maintaining our possessions in God. Verse 29 alludes to the fact that pageantry contributed to maintaining the peace!
> (Fischer and Griffing 1985, 39)

Verse twenty-nine certainly implies this fact: *"And the fear of God was on all the kingdoms of those countries when they heard that the LORD had fought against the enemies of Israel."*

THE PROPHETIC LINK BETWEEN DAVID AND THE SON OF DAVID

Prophetically illustrating the joy of the church when Christ returns, when we will usher back our King to reign, the men of

Judah in David's day marched out to the Jordan river to welcome David back and escort him into Jerusalem as their returning king:

> *So he swayed the hearts of all the men of Judah, just as the heart of one man, so that they sent this word to the king: "Return, you and all your servants!" Then the king returned and came to the Jordan. And Judah came to Gilgal, to go to meet the king, to escort the king across the Jordan.* (2 Sam. 19:14–15)

The coincidences between these two events, the return of David and the return of the Son of David, are too numerous to dismiss as accidental. Having been rejected by his own people, King David—Jesus' *"own did not receive Him"* (John 1:11)—as did his "Son" a thousand years later—ascended the Mount of Olives and disappeared from Jerusalem, leaving behind his faithful priests to tarry in Jerusalem with the presence of God (the ark) to encourage them until his return:

> *The king said also unto Zadok the priest, Art not thou a seer? return into the city in peace....Zadok therefore and Abiathar carried the ark of God again to Jerusalem: and they tarried there. And David went up by the ascent of mount Olivet.* (2 Sam. 15:27, 29–30 KJV)

Later, when it was time for him to return, the men of Judah marched out to the Jordan (an illustration of death?) to receive King David back again and conducted him back across the Jordan on a ferryboat (rising above death into resurrection life?) to return to Jerusalem to rule and reign again as king: *"And Judah came to Gilgal, to go to meet the king, to escort the king across the Jordan....Then a ferryboat went across to carry over the king's household"* (2 Sam. 19:15, 18).

When the church in these days celebrates the presence of our King of Kings and Lord of Lords by marching in processions of praise and worship, with our banners unfurled and our rejoicing manifested in dances of joy, we are welcoming His presence into our cities in greater and greater displays of glory. We are actually preparing the way for that great Day when we will usher back our returning King, the Lord Jesus Christ, to reign over the whole earth!

Chapter 14

The Invisible Becoming Visible

The physical universe has been created to illustrate the unseen realm of the kingdom of heaven: *"We do not look at the things which are seen, but at the things which are not seen; for the things which are seen are temporary, but the things which are not seen are eternal"* (2 Cor. 4:18).

What is seen manifests truth about the unseen, eternal realm. The physical universe exists to reveal truth about the invisible things of God. It was the invisible Spirit that brought forth visible matter. The spiritual created the physical; therefore, the natural realm takes form and meaning from the spiritual. This took place at Creation:

> And God said...light...and there was...
> And God said...sky...and it was so...
> And God said...land...and it was so...
> Then God said...plants...and it was so...
> And God said...sun, moon, and stars...and it was so...
> And God said...fish and birds...so God created...
> And God said...animals...and it was so...
> And God said...man...so God created....
>
> (See Genesis 1.)

The eternal God, who is spirit, spoke His creative word and by that Word brought into being the visible realm, a physical creation that originates in and takes its meaning from the eternal, spiritual realm. Therefore, the physical universe and our own bodies reflect and manifest the invisible glory of the unseen God.

Experiencing God's Power in Worship

For since the creation of the world God's invisible quali-
ties—his eternal power and divine nature—have been
clearly seen, being understood from what has been made.

(Rom. 1:20 NIV)

We understand the invisible from seeing the visible. We understand something of the eternal from seeing the temporal.
The physical reveals the heavenly, and the natural portrays the
spiritual. In fact, because we as human beings are limited to the
space-time realm in which we have been created, God, who is
Spirit, uses this natural world to reveal Himself and His glory:
"The spiritual did not come first, but the natural, and after that
the spiritual" (1 Cor. 15:46 NIV).

What a wonderful world we live in, where everything reveals the glory of God and contains physical manifestations of
God's eternal truth and existence! No wonder Jesus, the Word
made flesh, used the natural creation to reveal truth about
eternity. For that eternal Word intelligently brought forth the
creation with built-in illustrations of heavenly truth and reality,
which were later revealed by the teaching ministry of the Holy
Spirit.

It was not that Jesus cleverly looked around for earthly examples to illustrate the spiritual truths He was trying to convey,
as if to say to Himself, "Ah, there's a flock of sheep. What a
great example of My people. I think I'll use sheep as an illustration in My next sermon." The teaching ministry of Jesus was
much more awesome and fundamental than that.

Since Jesus was the creative Word of God, it means that
when sheep were created, they were made with you and me in
mind. God originally gave them their sheeplike nature to show
us ourselves. When Jesus appeared in human history, he simply
drew out the meaning, which was predesigned in the original
Creation. He told us He was the Good Shepherd (John 10:11).
He told us that as sheep know their shepherd's voice, so we
would know His (v. 4). He told us we were *"the sheep of His pas-*
ture" (Ps. 100:3). He told us He was the door into the sheepfold,
the church. (See John 10:1, 7.) He told us that His ministry was
to search for lost sheep. (See verses 1–18.)

All of these qualities were built into sheep at Creation to reveal truth about us. And this is so not only with sheep—all of creation has been predesigned in this way. Jesus simply drew out the original meaning hidden in the visible realm to teach us truth about the invisible, spiritual realm, when He spoke of vineyards, fig trees, fish, oxen, stars, rocks, bread, blood, serpents, storms, wind, sun, water, the sea, seeds, light, salt, leaven, swine, pearls, gold, ground, the harvest, plants, fruit, and more.

And spiritual truth is not just concealed in the physical creation, but in human history as well, as God progressively revealed truth about Himself and His plan of salvation in the events that occurred in the Old Testament. This abundance of revelation is so overwhelming that the New Testament writers were constantly reaching back into the history of the Old Testament, and into nature itself, for natural and historical illustrations of spiritual truth, which they then applied to Christ and His church. The following chart illustrates some of these spiritual applications:

HISTORY/ NATURE	NEW TESTAMENT REFERENCE	FULFILLMENT
Adam	Rom. 5:14; 1 Cor. 15:45–49	Christ
Isaac	Rom. 9:7–9; Heb. 11:17–18	Christ
Melchisedec	Heb. 5:5–10; 7:1–27	Christ
Joseph	Acts 7:9	Christ
Son of David	Rev. 5:5; 22:16; Mark 10:47; John 7:42; Matt. 21:9, 15	Christ
Seed of Abraham	Gal. 3:16	Christ
Bridegroom	Matt. 25:1–13; Luke 5:33–35	Christ
King	Matt. 2:2; John 1:49; 19:3, 19	Christ
Shepherd	John 10:1–18; 1 Pet. 2:25	Christ
High Priest	Heb. 4:14–16; 9:7–14	Christ
Lamb	John 1:29	Christ
Rock	Luke 6:48; Matt. 7:24–25; 1 Cor. 3:11; 10:4	Christ
Vine	John 15:1–7	Christ
Temple	John 2:13–21	Christ
Cornerstone	1 Pet. 2:4–6	Christ

Experiencing God's Power in Worship

Bread	John 6:31–51	Christ
Blood Sacrifice	Heb. 9:7–28; 10:11–12	Christ
Moses' Serpent	John 3:14–15	Christ
Bread	Matt. 15:26–27; Mark 6:41–44	Word of God
Manna	1 Cor. 10:3; John 6:31–35; 2 Cor. 8:15	Word of God
Seed	Matt. 13:18–23; Mark 4:14–20, 26	Word of God
Water	Eph. 5:26	Word of God
Sword	Eph. 6:17; Heb. 4:12	Word of God
Zion	Heb. 12:22–24; Rev. 14:1–5; Rom. 9:33	The church
Jerusalem	Gal. 4:26; Heb. 12:22–24	The church
Israel	Gal. 6:16; Rom. 9:6–8	The church
House of God	Eph. 2:19–22; 1 Tim. 3:15; 1 Pet. 2:5–10; Heb. 3:6	The church
Household	Matt. 24:42–51	The church
Temple	Eph. 2:19–22; Rev. 3:12	The church
Sheepfold	John 10:1–18	The church
Flock	Acts 20:28; 1 Pet. 5:2	The church
Vineyard	Matt. 21:33–43; Mark 12:1–11; Luke 20:9–16	The church
Olive Tree	Rom. 11:16–24	The church
Candlestick	Rev. 1:20	The church
Bride	Rev. 21:2	The church
Woman	2 John 1, 13; Rev. 12:1–6	The church
Farming	Matt. 13:24–30	Kingdom of God
Mustard Seed	Matt. 13:31–32	Kingdom of God
Leaven	Matt. 13:33	Kingdom of God
Treasure	Matt. 13:44	Kingdom of God
Pearl	Matt. 13:45–46	Kingdom of God
Fishnet	Matt. 13:47–50	Kingdom of God
David's Throne	Luke 1:32; Acts 2:30; Rom. 15:12	Kingdom of God
Water	John 4:10–15; 7:37–79	Holy Spirit
Wind	John 3:8	Holy Spirit
Firstfruit	Rom. 8:23	Holy Spirit
Promised Blessing	Gal. 3:14	Holy Spirit
Comforter	John 14:16–17	Holy Spirit
Dove	John 1:32–33	Holy Spirit
Fire	Luke 3:16; Acts 2:1–4	Holy Spirit
Red Sea	1 Cor. 10:1–2	Water Baptism
Circumcision	Col. 2:11–12	Water Baptism
The Flood	1 Pet. 3:20–21	Water Baptism
Sheep	Matt. 18:11–14; John 10:1–18; 21:15–17	Christians

Branches	John 15:1–8; Rom. 11:16–24	Christians
Stones	1 Pet. 2:5	Christians
Temples	1 Cor. 3:16; 6:19	Christians
Temple vessels	2 Tim. 2:20–21	Christians
Fish	Mark 1:16–18	People
Trees	Luke 3:9; 6:43–45	People
Sea	Rev. 17:15	People
Wheat	John 4:35	People
Harvest	Luke 10:2; John 4:35	People
Stewards	Luke 12:42–48; 1 Pet. 4:10	Ministers
Fishermen	Matt. 4:19; Mark 1:17	Ministers
Farmers	Matt. 21:33–43; Luke 20:9–16	Ministers
Laborers	Luke 10:2; John 4:35–38	Ministers
Oxen	1 Cor. 9:9–14	Ministers

The eternal Scripture contains wonderful examples and illustrations of God's eternal plan of the ages. As one is immersed in the details of the scriptural writings, wonderful patterns emerge, in which the glory of the foreknowledge of God is seen in the minutest details of the redemptive history of the people of God. Even by naming people and places, God has revealed glorious prophetic truths about the present and future. The following chart catalogs some of the many instances where names were given because of their historical or prophetic significance:

REFERENCE	NAME	MEANING
Gen. 3:20	Eve	life-giver
Gen. 5:2	Adam	show blood in the face
Gen. 5:29	Noah	rest, quietness
Gen. 11:9	Babel	confusion
Gen. 16:11	Ishmael	God will hear.
Gen. 16:14	Beer Lahai Roi	well of the living
Gen. 17:5	Abraham	father of a multitude
Gen. 21:3, 6	Isaac	laughter
Gen. 21:31	Beersheba	well of an oath
Gen. 22:14 KJV	Jehovahjireh	God will provide.
Gen. 25:25	Esau	rough
Gen. 25:26	Jacob	supplanter
Gen. 25:30	Edom	red
Gen. 26:20	Esek	strife, quarrel
Gen. 26:21	Sitnah	opposition, attack

Gen. 26:22	Rehoboth	to make room
Gen. 28:19	Bethel	house of God
Gen. 29:32	Reuben	behold, a son
Gen. 29:33	Simeon	hearing
Gen. 29:34	Levi	joined, united
Gen. 29:35	Judah	praise, extended hands
Gen. 30:6	Dan	judge
Gen. 30:8	Naphtali	wrestling
Gen. 30:11	Gad	invading troop
Gen. 30:13	Asher	happy, joyful
Gen. 30:18	Issachar	bringing a reward
Gen. 30:20	Zebulun	habitation
Gen. 30:24	Joseph	let him add
Gen. 31:48	Galeed	heap of testimony
Gen. 32:2	Mahanaim	two armies, companies
Gen. 32:28	Israel	He will prevail like God.
Gen. 32:30	Peniel	the face of God
Gen. 33:17	Succoth	booths
Gen. 35:7	El Bethel	the God of Bethel
Gen. 35:8	Allon Bachuth	oak of weeping
Gen. 35:18	Ben-Oni	son of my sorrow
Gen. 38:29	Pharez	breaking forth
Exod. 2:10	Moses	to draw out, rescue
Exod. 15:23	Marah	bitter
Exod. 16:31	Manna	What is it?
Exod. 17:7	Massah	testing, tempting
Exod. 17:7	Meribah	strife, quarrel
Exod. 17:15 KJV	Jehovahnissi	The Lord is my banner.
Num. 11:3	Taberah	burning
Num. 11:34	Kibroth Hattaavah	graves of lust
Num. 13:24	Eschol	cluster of grapes
Num. 21:3	Hormah	destruction
Josh. 5:9	Gilgal	to roll away
Josh. 7:26	Achor	trouble, to disturb
Judg. 2:4–5	Bochim	weepers
Judg. 6:24 KJV	Jehovahshalom	The Lord is peace.
Judg. 6:32	Jerubbaal	Let Baal contend.
Judg. 15:17	Ramath Lehi	hill of a jawbone
Judg. 18:12	Mahaneh Dan	camp of Dan
1 Sam. 4:21	Ichabod	The glory is gone.
1 Sam. 7:12	Ebenezer	stone of help
1 Sam. 23:28 KJV	Selahammahlekoth	rock of separation
2 Sam. 5:20	Baal Perazim	breaking out in war

2 Sam. 12:25	Jedidiah	beloved of the Lord
1 Kings 9:13	Cabul	sterile, worthless
2 Kings 18:4	Nehustan	a piece of brass
1 Chron. 4:9	Jabez	to sorrow, grieve
1 Chron. 7:23	Beriah	in trouble
1 Chron. 13:11	Perez Uzza	breach of Uzza
2 Chron. 20:26	Berachah	blessing, praise
Isa. 8:3	Maher-Shalal-Hash-Baz	hasting to the spoil
Isa. 62:4	Hephzibah	My delight is in her.
Isa. 62:4	Beulah	to marry
Jer. 20:3	Magor Missabib	fear of terror
Ezek. 20:29	Bamah	high place, elevation
Hos. 1:6	Lo-Ruhamah	not pitied
Hos. 1:9	Lo-Ammi	not my people
Matt. 1:21	Jesus	Jehovah saves.
Matt. 1:23	Emmanuel	God with us
Matt. 16:18	Peter	rock
Mark 5:9	Legion	regiment

Just an overview of the meanings of these biblical names is truly awe inspiring! When one studies the historical context of the giving of these names, tremendous revelation and even prophetic truth about the future is discovered. What a wonderful God we serve! What a glorious Creator, infinite in His wisdom and revelation! Nowhere is His awesome glory displayed more than in the intricacies of the human body. Should that be surprising, if we have been created in His very image? We see because He sees. We hear because He hears. We speak because He does:

He that planted the ear, shall he not hear? He that formed the eye, shall he not see?...He that teacheth man knowledge, shall not he know? (Ps. 94:9–10 KJV)

REFLECTIONS OF HIS IMAGE

Here we see the argument for the existence of God based upon analogy. If we have truly been created in His image, if we are in that sense a picture of Him, then we can study the picture in order to understand the One from whom it was developed! The lens of the creative Word has focused a likeness of God's

Being on the film of our human nature, so that we are an actual image and representation of God.

In our regenerated state, with the nature of Christ implanted in us, we become even more representative of the Lord. We are not only like Him by analogy in our physical bodies, but the Spirit of God also recreates the image of God in our spiritual beings as well:

> *But we all, with unveiled face, beholding as in a mirror the glory of the Lord, are being transformed into the same image from glory to glory.* (2 Cor. 3:18)

> *Do not lie to each other, since you have taken off your old self with its practices and have put on the new self, which is being renewed in knowledge in the image of its Creator.* (Col. 3:9–10 NIV)

> *And just as we have borne the likeness of the earthly man, so shall we bear the likeness of the man from heaven.* (1 Cor. 15:49 NIV)

> *But we know that when he appears, we shall be like him.* (1 John 3:2 NIV)

If we are *"like him"* and if we are His body, then the Spirit-filled man and the Spirit-filled church are visible expressions of the invisible God. When we are energized and motivated by His Spirit, we move, speak, and act as He desires, so that His eternal Word and will are visibly demonstrated through His body. We call this prophecy or prophetic action.

God has always manifested His will through His body, for the whole purpose of having a body is to visibly demonstrate to others the intent of the invisible person who inhabits it. By means of words and actions, we communicate to others the most complex concepts and meanings. By means of the slightest variations in facial expressions and body language and by the intricate nuances of our words and tone of voice, we communicate an amazing variety of meanings and intentions. So it is with God. He moved by His Spirit in times past to motivate men and women to speak His mind in prophetic words and to demonstrate His will in prophetic action. And He continues to do this today. This is what it means for the church to be His body on earth. The Spirit of God sets His body in motion, just as we set our bodies in motion whenever we want to say or do anything in the natural realm.

Chapter 15

Prophecy in Action

*W*hen God chooses to put His body in motion by speaking or moving through His people, we call it prophecy or prophetic action. Prophecy is simply God-initiated words or actions that communicate His mind, thoughts, and plans. The Bible is filled with such God-motivated speech and deeds.

In both Testaments, God spoke and acted prophetically through His servants to clearly communicate to us His will and truth. In addition to Spirit-initiated music, which provided an orchestration for prophetic song, God also choreographed His prophetic Word, pictured in dance and movement, as prophets were moved by the Spirit to act out in visible ways the mind and purposes of the Almighty. God understands the wisdom contained in the simple proverb, A picture is worth a thousand words. In our modern generation, so media-oriented and deadened by the bombardment of endless words, He desires to put His Word into action today, so that He can capture our minds and hearts through the eye-gate as well as the ear-gate.

The proliferation of the arts in prophetic worship today to communicate truth through spontaneous movement and visual images is evidence that the Lord is again releasing His prophetic anointing in visible acts, as He did in biblical times. He originally expressed His *"eternal power and divine nature"* (Rom. 1:20 NIV) through the visible realm of creation. His *"invisible qualities...have been clearly seen, being understood from what has been made"* (v. 20 NIV). He is still manifesting His Word in creative, visible ways.

Prophets in both Old and New Testament times were well-known for their unusual actions. In fact, their strange deeds often mystified people who had no grasp of the spiritual realm. At times, their actions must have seemed ridiculous, even as they sometimes do today!

ELISHA AND THE ARROWS

When Jehoash, king of Israel, visited Elisha on his sick bed one day, the king did not know what awaited him. *"Get a bow and some arrows"* (2 Kings 13:15 NIV), the prophet told him. Then Elisha put his hand on the king's hands. *"Open the east window,"* Elisha said, and *"shoot!"* (v. 17 NIV). As the king released the arrow, the prophet interpreted what the action meant: *"The Lord's arrow of victory, the arrow of victory over Aram!"* (v. 17 NIV). What? Shoot an arrow out of a bedroom window and get the victory over a nation? It couldn't be! Then things became even stranger. The prophet asked Jehoash to take the other arrows and beat them on the floor. You don't use arrows as clubs! The king hesitated but knew he should probably obey what Elisha said, because, after all, he was a prophet.

Outwardly obedient, he inwardly doubted the significance of what he was doing, and he certainly did not act in faith. Half-heartedly, just to please the prophet, he tentatively struck the floor with the arrows three times. *"You should have struck the ground five or six times"* (v. 19 NIV), Elisha thundered angrily, *"Then you would have defeated Aram and completely destroyed it. But now you will defeat it only three times"* (v. 19 NIV). And Aram or Syria survived to later attack Israel in the future.

How unfair to blame a king who was totally dense to the realm of the Spirit for not enthusiastically believing that there was some divine connection between how he beat Elisha's bedroom floor with arrows and the events of international war! Yet so is the God of the Bible. So is our God.

Other prophets acted out messages from the Lord to Israel in such clear terms that there was no escaping God's intentions. Once, the Lord wanted to tell Israel that their sins and iniquities had hidden His face from them, and instead of seeing Him, they were going to experience His judgment. How was He going to do this? For generations, He had sent prophets who had spoken to Israel over and over again, and it seemed that just to tell them one more time would have had no more impact than before. What was God to do? He decided to act out His prophetic message in such a way that the people themselves would ask the question, "What does this mean?"

EZEKIEL AND THE MODEL OF JERUSALEM

"Make a model of the city of Jerusalem," God told Ezekiel. "Erect battering rams and enemy camps around it, and portray the impending destruction of the city. Then lie on your left side next to this model, and put an iron pan like a wall between your face and the city." Ezekiel was to do this in a public place, so that the people of Jerusalem would see what he was doing. And they had plenty of time to get the message. "I am going to ask you to do this one day for each year of the sin of Israel—for 390 days," the Lord said.

"Then turn over on your right side, and lay there another 40 days, one day for each year of the sin of Judah," the Lord continued. And it got worse! "Store up enough food and water to ration out a certain limited amount for each day, and you can use your own excrement to cook your meals with." This was too much for Ezekiel. "I can't do that!" he cried. "Nothing unclean has ever entered my mouth." "Very well, then," replied the Lord. "You can use cow manure instead" (Ezek. 4:1–15, author's paraphrase).

What was God trying to do? He was trying to get His message across, a message that His people had tired of hearing. Now He was going to visibly act it out before their eyes. The interpretation of Ezekiel's actions was clear. Because of the iniquity of the city of Jerusalem, God was allowing its enemies to lay siege against it. And because of their sins, the face of the Lord was hidden from them by the iron wall of judgment that was coming. Even the limited rations Ezekiel ate and drank every day were a prophetic picture of the coming attack against Jerusalem when *"food and water* [would] *be scarce"* (Ezek. 4:17 NIV).

And the grossness of using excrement to cook food was a powerful way of showing Israel that they were feeding on things that should have been eliminated.

When the men of Judah passed by Ezekiel the first day, they saw this strange prophet lying on his side with an iron pan between his face and the model city of Jerusalem, with over a year's worth of food and water stored beside him. "What does this mean?" they wondered. All Ezekiel had to do was to give them the prophetic interpretation! God had commanded him *"with bared arm [to] prophesy against her"* (Ezek. 4:7 NIV). Ezekiel's face had become, by a dramatic parable, the face of the Lord. The iron pan hiding his face from the model city of Jerusalem symbolized the coming judgment because of the sin of Israel that had hidden the face of the Lord from the city.

Imagine the impact of this acted prophecy day after day, week after week, month after month. To be sure, by the end of one year and seventy days, everyone in Jerusalem had heard the message. God continued to ask Ezekiel to do more prophetic acts, even after the 430 days of portraying the destruction of Jerusalem. He asked him to shave off his hair and beard and divide his hair into three parts. He was to burn one-third of his hair inside the city; one-third was to be taken outside the city and smitten with a sword; and one-third was to be thrown to the winds. (See Ezekiel 5:1–2.) Why do such a thing? The interpretation of this action was clear:

> *A third of your people will die of the plague or perish by famine inside you; a third will fall by the sword outside your walls; and a third I will scatter to the winds and pursue with drawn sword.* (Ezek. 5:12 NIV)

EZEKIEL AND THE TUNNEL

Another time, God asked Ezekiel to physically dig through the wall of Jerusalem—an incredibly difficult job! He was to be ready to escape from the city with all his belongings in a pack on his back and with his eyes covered up. When the men of Judah asked him what he was doing, he was to explain that because of the attack of the Babylonians that was coming against Jerusalem, the king of Judah would have to escape by digging through the wall of the city with his treasured belongings on his back, and he would then be captured and carried off to the land of Babylon, even though *"he shall not see it"* (Ezek. 12:13). What an amazing prophetic act! Jeremiah records the fulfillment of this acted prophecy, even down to the last detail: *"Then he put out Zedekiah's eyes and bound him with bronze shackles to take him to Babylon"* (Jer. 39:7 NIV).

HOSEA AND THE PROSTITUTE

Many other prophets in Israel demonstrated in a visual way what the invisible God was trying to declare to His people. Hosea had to marry a former prostitute and try to get her to remain faithful to him:

> Go, show your love to your wife again, though she is loved by another and is an adulteress. Love her as the LORD loves the Israelites, though they turn to other gods.
> (Hos. 3:1 NIV)

ISAIAH AND HIS NAKEDNESS

Isaiah had to publicly run around *"stripped and barefoot"* (Isa. 20:2 NIV) as a sign against the nations of Egypt and Cush, that just as he had done, *"the king of Assyria [would] lead away stripped and barefoot the Egyptian captives and Cushite exiles"* (v. 4 NIV).

AGABUS AND THE BELT

This kind of prophetic action is not limited to the Old Testament. Imagine what would happen in some churches today if someone approached the platform, took the pastor's belt off, and tied up his hands and feet with it. That is what the prophet Agabus did to the apostle Paul in Caesarea, as he explained his own prophetic action:

> After we had been there a number of days, a prophet named Agabus came down from Judea. Coming over to us,

171

he took Paul's belt, tied his own hands and feet with it and said, "The Holy Spirit says, 'In this way the Jews of Jerusalem will bind the owner of this belt and will hand him over to the Gentiles.'"   (Acts 21:10–11 NIV)

If the Spirit of the Lord moved so clearly in biblical times to act out and demonstrate His messages, is it surprising to hear that the Lord is moving in these same ways today to motivate His people by His invisible Spirit to clearly demonstrate and act out the Word of the Lord? Truly, a picture is worth a thousand words.

WORD PICTURES

Sometimes a picture can be simply described without being acted out physically with the same effect. Such a verbal word picture creates in the mind's eye what an action would have created for the natural eye. Thus, all of the word pictures and parables in the ministry of Jesus and the prophetic pictures and dreams in the Bible are examples of God's ability to capture our minds by means of visions and illustrative parables. Often in Scripture, God shows the prophet a picture of something and then asks him what it means. The Lord then follows with the interpretation:

The LORD showed me two baskets of figs....One basket had very good figs;...the other basket had very poor figs....Then the LORD asked me, "What do you see, Jeremiah?" "Figs," I answered. "The good ones are very good, but the poor ones are so bad they cannot be eaten."   (Jer. 24:1–3 NIV)

Such a prophetic picture presented to the prophet was just as clear and meaningful as if two real baskets of figs had actually been placed before him. But what did it mean? *"Like these good figs, I regard as good the exiles from Judah....But like the poor figs...so will I deal with Zedekiah"* (Jer. 24:5, 8 NIV).

The Bible is replete with such examples. How many times do the prophets declare, "The Lord showed me this" or "The Lord showed me that"? Then they explain the meaning that the Lord gave them concerning the vision. This happened so often

172

in Scripture that prophets actually became known as seers. The words *prophet* and *seer* are used interchangeably, because a prophet became known as a person who sees the invisible realm of the Spirit and to whom God makes known His Word by means of dreams and visions.

Daniel, one of the greatest prophets in the Bible, was described as a man who *"could understand visions and dreams of all kinds"* (Dan. 1:17 NIV). In one of his prophetic visions, the Lord showed him a ram with two horns charging toward the west and then a goat with one horn charging toward the east. They attacked each other, and the goat was victorious and became very great. Then its single horn was broken off, and four other horns took its place in four different locations *"toward the four winds of heaven"* (Dan. 8:8 NIV).

What could this mean? The Lord explained it this way:

The two-horned ram that you saw represents the kings of Media and Persia. The shaggy goat is the king of Greece, and the large horn between his eyes is the first king. The four horns that replaced the one that was broken off represent four kingdoms that will emerge from his nation but will not have the same power. (Dan. 8:20–22 NIV)

What prophetic accuracy! After the death of Daniel, the two-pronged kingdom of the Medes and Persians were attacked by Alexander the Great, the famed king of Greece. Medo-Persia was destroyed, and the empire of Alexander the Great conquered all the Near Eastern kingdoms of his day. After his death, his empire fragmented into four parts, each governed by one of his previous generals, but none of these four kingdoms that splintered off ever equaled the power of the former Greek empire.

Another example of the use of word pictures occurred when the apostle John was taken into heaven itself. He was shown all manner of beasts and horns, which represented kingdoms of the earth. (See Revelation 5:6.) The Lord communicated to him truth concerning the future reign of the kingdom of God over all earthly kingdoms.

We believe that even today the Lord is communicating eternal truth and giving prophetic direction to His church by means of visions or prophetic acts. What He wishes to communicate to us is presented either to our natural eyes, in the form of visible action, or to our minds' eyes, in the form of word pictures in visionary form. The culmination of these prophetic presentations is the interpretation of His Word, which gives us the understanding and explanation of what we have seen.

Chapter 16

Spiritual Warfare

Jesus taught us to pray, *"Your will be done on earth as it is in heaven"* (Matt. 6:10), because this prayer agrees with the Father's heart. He wants to bring the life, power, and glory of heaven into the misery, sin, and despair of the earth, to redeem lives and restore them to the glorious image and will of God.

When Christ came to take away the sin of the world, a cosmic change occurred behind the scenes in the realm of eternity. Satan was defeated, his kingdom was plundered, death was overcome, and as a result of the resurrection and ascension of Christ to the right hand of the Father, paradise in heaven was opened to all the men and women of faith of all the ages past.

This happened in the unseen realm. But the change began to be manifested in the earth when the Holy Spirit was poured out upon the disciples on the Day of Pentecost. Peter was able to say to the people of Israel, "These miraculous tongues of fire that you have seen and the miraculous tongues of the nations that you have heard are evidences here and now that Jesus Christ has been raised from the dead and has been exalted to the throne of God. The living Christ is doing these things now!" (See Acts 2:14–36.)

> *God has raised this Jesus to life, and we are all witnesses of the fact. Exalted to the right hand of God, he has received from the Father the promised Holy Spirit and has poured out what you now see and hear.* (Acts 2:32–33 NIV)

Ever since the glorious beginning of the early church, God has been continuing to do things that people of the earth can see

175

and hear, both by transforming lives from the kingdom of darkness into His marvelous kingdom of light and by displaying His glory through His body in gifts and manifestations of the Holy Spirit.

By means of spiritual warfare, the power of God in the heavenly realm invades the kingdoms of this world in strategic places at strategic times to bind and drive out the resistant forces of darkness, which are called principalities and powers (Eph. 6:12), and to release and manifest the power of the kingdom of God on earth. Flashes of the power of the kingdom of God appeared in the life and ministry of Jesus Christ. Jesus said, *"If I cast out demons with the finger of God, surely the kingdom of God has come upon you"* (Luke 11:20). Life and power poured out of His hands and mouth as the lame were healed, the deaf heard, the blind saw, and the dead were raised to life. Christ then committed His power and authority into the hands of His church: *"And as you go, preach, saying, 'The kingdom of heaven is at hand.' Heal the sick, cleanse the lepers, raise the dead, cast out demons"* (Matt. 10:7–8).

And Jesus said to His disciples, *"All authority has been given to Me in heaven and on earth. Go therefore and make disciples of all the nations"* (Matt. 28:18–19).

WE ARE HIS HANDS

In order for us to release the power of the kingdom of God on earth, we must be in synchronization with the will and purpose of God in the heavenly realm. When the unseen power of the Holy Spirit desires to move in the earth in a specific time and place, we, as His ministers on earth, need to mirror or act out visibly on earth what the Father's will is in heaven. We touch people He wants to touch. We heal people He wants to heal. We speak to people He wants to reach. Jesus patterned for us this kind of ministry, which linked His actions on earth with His Father's will in heaven: *"For I have come down from heaven, not to do My own will, but the will of Him that sent me"* (John 6:38). *"I do nothing of Myself; but as My Father taught Me, I speak these things"* (John 8:28). To the Jews who were persecuting Him, Jesus said,

The Son can do nothing of Himself, but what He sees the Father do; for whatever He does, the Son also does in like manner. For the Father loves the Son, and shows Him all things that He Himself does. (John 5:19–20)

Jesus moved upon earth in perfect harmony and synchronization with His Father in heaven. As the invisible Spirit moved around Him, Jesus visibly moved with it, stretching out His hands to heal, preaching and expressing the wonderful works of God in ways that could be seen and heard. This is the challenge and ministry for the church today: to be so led and empowered by the Holy Spirit that what we do on earth reflects the will and purpose of our Father who is in heaven.

The church is to be the link between the visible earth and the invisible heaven. The body of Christ on earth manifests and does what the Spirit of God in heavenly places wills to be done.

The desire of our Father is to seek and to save the lost and to bless the whole earth through His church. He really does not want to take us to heaven as much as He wants to manifest His will and the reign of His kingdom here on earth:

My prayer is not that you take them out of the world but that you protect them from the evil one....I pray also for those who will believe in me through their message, that all of them may be one....May they also be in us so that the world may believe that you have sent me.
(John 17:15, 20–21 NIV)

A WAR IS GOING ON

Our focus, along with that of Jesus and the Father, is to see the will of God done here on earth as it is being done in heaven and to see the kingdom of heaven mightily impact the earth. Of course, this involves the restoration of extravagant, glorious, and beautiful worship, so that what is expressed here on earth in our churches can come as close as possible to displaying the glory, color, brilliance, and sound of worship that has always existed around the throne of God in heaven. But it also involves warfare, as the powers of God in heaven engage and drive back the powers of darkness here on earth.

Experiencing God's Power in Worship

We know too little about these titanic struggles, but they are apparently linked to our rather feeble efforts at prayer and worship. If we only saw God's perspective on our prayer and worship, we would be much more faithful to these ministries.

THE POWER OF PRAYER

Daniel once fasted and prayed for twenty-one days, seemingly fruitlessly, unaware of the cosmic struggle in the heavenly realm, which was set in motion by his prayers, until the messenger of the Lord finally arrived and explained to him the full story of what had happened:

> *Do not be afraid, Daniel. Since the first day that you set your mind to gain understanding and to humble yourself before God, your words were heard, and I have come in response to them. But the prince of the Persian kingdom resisted me twenty-one days. Then Michael, one of the chief princes, came to help me, because I was detained there with the king of Persia. Now I have come to you to explain to you what will happen to your people in the future.*
> (Dan. 10:12–14 NIV)

What a revelation! Here was a man wrestling in prayer and fasting for three weeks, not feeling any answers or release, unaware that above him in the heavenly realms over his nation was a pitched battle between the forces of Jehovah and the resistant forces of the demonic strongholds over Persia. It took the messenger of God twenty-one days to break through this opposition to reach Daniel with his answer. And he had to have help! But the most amazing revelation of all is that the whole cosmic struggle that engaged the forces of light and darkness was set in motion by Daniel's prayers. It all began the very first day he set his heart to seek God.

Little does the church understand these things today. But we desperately need to learn about them and be taught by the Holy Spirit and by revelation from the Word of God. We are engaged in a great warfare between the flesh and the spirit and between the powers of darkness and the powers of the kingdom of God, and we desperately need help in our struggle.

Praise God, help is available! It sometimes comes by prophetic revelation during powerful times of praise and worship. As the Spirit and presence of God is released by worshiping the Lord *"in spirit and truth"* (John 4:24), the Holy Spirit can bring direction for future strategy in a gift of prophecy, either spoken or sung, which shows us how to pray, intercede, or act in agreement with the will of God. In that way, our efforts on earth are coordinated with the will of God in heaven.

SEEK GOD'S DIRECTION

A beautiful example of this is found in the life of King David, who, because he learned this principle, never lost a battle. David had previously defeated the Philistines by simply asking God, *"Shall I go and attack these Philistines?"* (1 Sam. 23:2). And the Lord had answered him, *"Go and attack the Philistines....For I will deliver the Philistines into your hand"* (vv. 2, 4). But later, when they returned to attack Israel, rather than assume he could defeat them one more time and rush back into battle, David did a wise thing, which is a principle of spiritual warfare: he inquired of the Lord again and did not depend upon the strategy of his past successes to determine the will of God for the future.

It is imperative that we know God's mind on each strategic move we make. It was very wise that David sought the Lord again, because God had a different answer this time: *"Do not go"* (2 Sam. 5:23 NIV). Instead, they were to circle around behind a grove of mulberry, or balsam, trees and wait until they heard a *"sound of marching in the tops of the balsam trees"* (v. 24 NIV). Then they were to *"move out to battle, because that will mean God has gone out in front of* [them] *to strike the Philistine army"* (1 Chron. 14:15 NIV).

Not surprisingly, David and his men won a decisive battle because they acted in harmony with the power of God in the heavenly realm. What an important truth! If we move on earth in concert with the hosts of the Lord in heaven, our earthly efforts are buttressed and enhanced by the power of God fighting for us in the heavenly realm, and wonderful victories can occur.

TRUST COMPLETELY IN GOD

King Jehoshaphat also experienced great help from the invasion of heavenly forces in his earthly struggle against the kings of Ammon, Moab, and Mount Seir (Edom). In a time of fear and uncertainty about how to fight their enemies, the whole nation prayed and sought the Lord for help. God answered them by speaking to them through His prophetic Spirit in the mouth of Jahaziel:

> *Do not be afraid or discouraged because of this vast army. For the battle is not yours, but God's....You will not have to fight this battle. Take up your positions; stand firm and see the deliverance the LORD will give you.*
>
> (2 Chron. 20:15, 17 NIV)

The king believed this prophetic word so wholeheartedly that he put singers out in front of the army to praise the Lord for the victory, as they marched to engage their enemies (v. 21). And a marvelous thing happened, which is at the heart of spiritual warfare. Because they believed the prophetic word and were strategically at the right place at the right time, the Lord was able to send *"ambushes"* (v. 22) from heaven against their enemies, and they destroyed each other before Israel ever arrived on the scene! (See verses 22–25.)

Our spiritual warfare can be frightening, especially if we cannot easily see the unseen forces of God in the heavens surrounding us. Jehoshaphat had to have enough faith in the prophetic Word of God to trust that Word implicitly, and he demonstrated his faith by sending out singers in front of the army.

PRAY FOR SPIRITUAL EYESIGHT

Certainly, in these days, the church of Jesus Christ needs greater vision and understanding in the realms of spiritual warfare so that our earthly efforts can coordinate with God's heavenly strategies to produce great victories here on earth. In this way, the kingdom of God can expand and come into greater manifestation before all nations.

In order to achieve effectiveness in spiritual warfare, we need help from the Lord to remove our spiritual blindness to the heavenly realm. Is it possible for us to become more aware of the hosts of God all around us, so that we are not so afraid? If we can live as the prophet Elisha did, we can achieve this goal and never be thrown into fear and turmoil by our circumstances. Let us take a look at what he did.

The Syrian army had come to his town to kill him, for his prophetic insight into their battle plans had repeatedly saved the king of Israel from their attacks. So they wanted to kill the source of these "leaks." The Syrian army surrounded Elisha's house in Dothan. The next morning, Elisha's servant awoke to discover their plight and ran to the prophet in panic, *"Oh, my lord, what shall we do?"* (2 Kings 6:15 NIV). Can we not identify with this man in his fear?

Elisha calmly answered his servant, *"Don't be afraid ....Those who are with us are more than those who are with them"* (v. 16 NIV). "What?" cried the servant. "Are you crazy? There's only you and me here!" he must have thought. "And there's thousands of Syrians out there! How can there be more with us than with them?" What was the problem? Simply that the servant was seeing only the natural realm. On just the earthly plane of existence, they were outnumbered thousands to two. But Elisha was seeing more than the natural realm. He prayed, *"O LORD, open his eyes so he may see* [the whole truth]*"* (v. 17 NIV). *"Then the LORD opened the servant's eyes, and he looked and saw the hills full of horses and chariots of fire all around Elisha"* (v. 17 NIV).

Oh, may we have the Lord open our eyes in this day, so that we may be able to see the whole picture! May we be aware of the angelic hosts of the Lord that surround us all the time! The chariots of fire were there all along, but until Elisha's servant had his eyes opened to see the heavenly realm as well as the earthly, he did not see the whole picture; consequently, he was living in fear.

EXPERIENCE A "DOUBLE PORTION"

Could this be part of the meaning of inheriting the *"double portion"* (2 Kings 2:9) of the Holy Spirit? Could it mean that we are able to see both the heavenly and the earthly realms at the same time, so that we may more fearlessly coordinate our actions with the will of God, even as Jesus was able to do? Earlier in his life, when Elisha had been asked by Elijah what he really wanted, the young prophet had astounded the prophetic veteran when he boldly proclaimed, *"Let me inherit a double portion of your spirit"* (v. 9 NIV). Elijah replied, *"You have asked a difficult thing...yet if you see me when I am taken from you, it will be yours"* (v. 10 NIV).

What did he mean, *"If you see me when I am taken"*? Precisely this, that if Elisha was able to see into the heavenly realm to see the chariot of fire that would come catch Elijah into heaven itself, then his request for the *"double portion"* of the Holy Spirit would be granted. Or perhaps more to the point, if his request for the double portion of the Holy Spirit had actually been granted, then he would be able to see into the heavenly realm and actually discern the chariot of fire coming out of heaven to catch away his master. Having a *"double portion"* of the Holy Spirit seems to involve this kind of double vision, the ability to see the realms of heaven and earth simultaneously.

Because Elisha had actually received this double portion of the Holy Spirit, he did twice as many miracles as Elijah did, and the ones he performed were much greater. For example, when Elijah multiplied the widow's oil, there was always only enough for the next meal, truly a "bottom of the barrel" ministry:

> *The jar of flour will not be used up and the jug of oil will not run dry until the day the LORD gives rain on the land....The jar of flour was not used up and the jug of oil did not run dry.* (1 Kings 17:14, 16 NIV)

When it was Elisha's turn to multiply a widow's oil, there was so much oil overflowing that she was able to fill every vessel she could find!

> *Elisha said, "Go around and ask all your neighbors for empty jars. Don't ask for just a few....Pour oil into all the jars....Go, sell the oil and pay your debts. You and your sons can live on what is left."* (2 Kings 4:3–4, 7 NIV)

When Elijah's life was threatened by Jezebel, he ran away in fear:

Now Ahab told Jezebel everything Elijah had done and how he had killed all the prophets with the sword. So Jezebel sent a messenger to Elijah to say, "May the gods deal with me, be it ever so severely, if by this time tomorrow I do not make your life like that of one of them." Elijah was afraid and ran for his life. (1 Kings 19:1–3 NIV)

When Elisha's life was threatened by king Jehoash, he calmly sat in his house, and God showed him by the Spirit how to avoid the coming attack of the king. Within twenty-four hours, through the word of Elisha, the whole city of Samaria was delivered from its famine.

Now Elisha was sitting in his house, and the elders were sitting with him. The king sent a messenger ahead, but before he arrived, Elisha said to the elders, "Don't you see how this murderer is sending someone to cut off my head? Look, when the messenger comes, shut the door and hold it shut against him."...Elisha said, "Hear the word of the LORD....About this time tomorrow, a seah of flour will sell for a shekel and two seahs of barley for a shekel at the gate of Samaria." (2 Kings 6:32; 7:1 NIV)

Today, we need to experience this *"double portion"* (2 Kings 2:9) of the Holy Spirit more than ever. The church is facing monumental opposition and the challenge of not only maintaining what we have, but also advancing into the territory held by the Enemy and reclaiming it for the kingdom of God. In order to accomplish these things, we will need the ability to effectively coordinate our efforts on earth with the great powers of God available to us in the heavenly realm.

Chapter 17

Joshua and David

Israel was approaching the Jordan River. Beyond it lay the land of milk and honey, promised to Abraham over four hundred years earlier. (See Genesis 15:13–16.) Most of their lives had been spent in the desert, wandering, circling from encampment to encampment, changing locations over thirty times in the forty years it had taken them to get from Egypt to Canaan. (See Numbers 33.) They experienced forty years of frustration—forty years of faithful endurance—forty years to go an eleven days' journey (Deut. 1:2)!

During their wilderness wanderings, the Israelites rehearsed the stories of their fathers, who had seen the miracles of deliverance from Egypt: the blood of the Passover Lamb put on the doors of their houses, the parting of the waters of the Red Sea where their enemies were destroyed, the pillar of cloud and fire, the manna from heaven, the miraculous water from the rock.

They wondered when they would experience the fulfillment of the Word of the Lord about dispossessing the nations of Canaan and inheriting their land of milk and honey. As they marched and awaited their time of conquest, however, something else was developing. The iniquity of the Amorites was increasing to a point where God could rightfully allow Israel to utterly destroy them:

> *Know for certain that your descendants will be strangers in a country not their own, and they will be enslaved and mistreated four hundred years....In the fourth generation your descendants will come back here, for the sin of the Amorites has not yet reached its full measure.*
>
> (Gen. 15:13, 16 NIV)

Experiencing God's Power in Worship

The tares and the wheat were both maturing, Israel and the Amorites, the church and the world together. They were both growing *"together until the harvest"* (Matt. 13:30).

When the fruit of wickedness was ripe, God allowed His people to conquer Canaan with the sword and take possession of their promised inheritance in the earth. They approached the Jordan River and waited for their next instructions. Joshua told them,

> *And they commanded the people, saying, When ye see the ark of the covenant of the LORD your God, and the priests the Levites bearing it, then ye shall remove from your place, and go after it. Yet there shall be a space between you and it, about two thousand cubits by measure: come not near unto it, that ye may know the way by which ye must go: for ye have not passed this way heretofore.*
> (Josh. 3:3–4 KJV)

The stage was set. The people of God were to follow the presence of God, associated with the ark of the covenant, but they were to stay *"about two thousand cubits* [original Hebrew wording]*"* behind it.

THE NEW ISRAEL

The Christian church is now approaching the end of its wilderness journey. In front of the church is the inheritance promised to it of possessing the nations of the earth (the land of milk and honey):

> *You are My Son, today I have begotten You. Ask of Me, and I will give You the nations for Your inheritance, and the ends of the earth for Your possession.* (Ps. 2:7–8)

The whole history of the church has been spent wandering in the wilderness of unfulfillment, going from stage to stage in the plan of God. The church has broken camp and moved on with God countless times in its two thousand years of history. That history has included two thousand years of frustration, two thousand years of faithful endurance, and two thousand years to go a seemingly short distance to spiritual maturity and authority. Although it has always been so close to fulfillment, nevertheless, it has been so far.

The church can look back on its glorious beginnings in the book of Acts and rehearse the miracles of its deliverance from this world (Egypt): how it was saved by the blood of the Lamb of God (the blood on the doors of the houses); how it experienced the cleansing power of the waters of baptism (the Red Sea) where the power of the old life was canceled (the drowning of the Egyptians); and how it received the baptism of the Holy Spirit (the pillar of cloud and fire), the revealed Word of God (manna from heaven), and the outpoured Holy Spirit (water from the rock).

And the church still wonders when it will experience the fulfillment of the Word of the Lord concerning inheriting the nations of the earth. For two thousand years, the church has been waiting to mature and for the iniquity of the earth to become full and ripe for judgment.

"A Day Is Like a Thousand Years"

The church approaches its transition into the fullness of kingdom authority and power (crossing the Jordan) and awaits its instructions. Jesus (the Greek word for Joshua) tells us through the interpretation of the details of the days of Joshua: "Stay two thousand paces (cubits) behind the presence of the Lord, which has gone before you across the Jordan (death)." No other generation of the church has ever gone this way before: you *"have not passed this way heretofore"* (Josh. 3:4 KJV). The Hebrew word for *"heretofore"* means simply "during the last two days" (during yesterday and the day before yesterday). *"With the Lord a day is like a thousand years, and a thousand years are like a day"* (2 Pet. 3:8 NIV).

Thus two days in God's calendar is the equivalent of two thousand years. Two thousand cubits after the ark entered the Jordan, the rest of the people of God were to follow. Could this mean that two thousand years after Christ conquered death and entered into His full kingdom authority at the right hand of God that His people would follow Him into resurrection life and

187

power and would possess the kingdoms of this world (Canaan)? Could it mean that the people of God would follow Christ into an experience of resurrection life and power, which has not occurred in any other generation of the church (you *"have not passed this way heretofore"*) at the culmination of these last two thousand years?

Other details in the crossing of the Jordan seem to confirm this interpretation. The first to enter the river were the priests who carried the ark, and as their feet touched the river, the water stopped flowing from as far away as the city of Adam:

> *As soon as the priests who carried the ark reached the Jordan and their feet touched the water's edge, the water from upstream stopped flowing. It piled up in a heap a great distance away, at a town called Adam.* (Josh. 3:15–16 NIV)

The ark represents the glory of God, fully manifested in Jesus Christ. As Christ went into His Jordan, the waters of death that had been flowing from as far away as Adam were stopped. Death was swallowed up in victorious life! Jesus passed through His Jordan of death into His glorious resurrection life and authority. After His resurrection, He was able to say, *"All authority has been given to Me in heaven and on earth"* (Matt. 28:18).

CHRIST IS THE FIRSTFRUIT

The New Testament declares that Jesus is only the first of many to enter into this fullness of life and power. He is the Firstfruit, and others will follow (two thousand years after Him?):

> *But Christ has indeed been raised from the dead, the firstfruits of those who have fallen asleep....For as in Adam all die, so in Christ all will be made alive. But each in his own turn: Christ, the firstfruits; then, when he comes, those who belong to him.* (1 Cor. 15:20, 22–23 NIV)

Christ is to be the Firstborn among many brothers. *"For those God foreknew he also predestined to be conformed to the likeness*

188

of his Son, that he might be the firstborn among many brothers" (Rom. 8:29 NIV).

Is there a generation of the church who are going to follow Christ into His kingdom's fullness of authority and power two thousand years after His earthly ministry (following the ark at a distance of *"about two thousand cubits"*)? (See Joshua 3:3–4.)

Are the waters of death that have been flowing at *"a great distance"* (Josh. 3:16 NIV) from Adam going to be *"cut off"* (v. 16), so that a generation can pass over the Jordan (death) into the fullness of resurrection life that no other generation of the church has been allowed to experience? *"You have not passed this way before"* (v. 4).

THE TWELVE STONES

When the people passed over the Jordan on dry ground, before the waters returned again, they took twelve stones from the riverbed, which had been covered over by water. These stones were placed on the opposite shore in the land of Canaan. Do we see here a picture of a recovery of the powerful New Testament apostolic ministry, which has been covered by the waters of death for two thousand years?

> *Take for yourselves twelve stones from here, out of the midst of the Jordan, from the place where the priests' feet stood firm. You shall carry them over with you....When your children ask in time to come, saying, "What do these stones mean to you?" Then you shall answer them that the waters of the Jordan were cut off before the ark of the covenant of the LORD.* (Josh. 4:3, 6–7)

One thing is certain: the church must have great faith in these last days to inherit all the promises of God and see the nations of this world *"become the kingdoms of our Lord and of His Christ"* (Rev. 11:15). We must receive greater faith through understanding more revealed truth from the Word of God than any other generation of the church. By the grace of God, are we equal to the challenge of our generation and ready for the plan of God, which is ready to be revealed in our immediate future?

ENEMIES IN HIGH PLACES

King David had this kind of faith. In his day, he was able to drive out his enemies from a stronghold that no other generation, not even Joshua's, had ever been able to permanently dispossess. The Jebusites had been entrenched in the high place of Jerusalem for so many years that no one ever thought it could be any different. After all, even the great military might of Judah in the days of Joshua had failed to drive them out:

> *As for the Jebusites, the inhabitants of Jerusalem, the children of Judah could not drive them out; but the Jebusites dwell with the children of Judah at Jerusalem to this day.* (Josh. 15:63)

And even though at times Israel had been able to defeat them in battle, no one could permanently dislodge them from their fortress. It became easy for Israel to accept the fact that having the Jebusite stronghold in the high place of the land was just the way things were. They came to accept it.

These enemies were in their high place, and the people of God just had to learn to coexist with them. The Jebusites remained in their stronghold all during the days of Joshua, all during the reign of the twelve judges. No one could touch them, not even Samson or Gideon or Deborah or Barak. The reign of the first king of Israel, Saul, came and went, and still they were there.

FAITH TO DEFEAT A GIANT

Then David came on the scene. This man's faith was so great that he believed no one could withstand the Lord. Even as a young lad, he was not impressed at all with Goliath's size or strength. After all, who was he, compared with...God! David asked, *"Who is this uncircumcised Philistine, that he should defy the armies of the living God?"* (1 Sam. 17:26). Through his faith, David defeated the giant and delivered the entire nation.

190

Joshua and David

As David ascended the throne of Israel much later in his life, following the death of Saul, when all the tribes invited him to rule over their entire kingdom, his great faith went into action once again. What was his first act as the new king over the newly united tribes? He fixed his eyes on the Jebusite stronghold:

> *When all the elders of Israel had come to King David at Hebron, he made a compact with them at Hebron before the LORD, and they anointed David king over Israel, as the LORD had promised through Samuel. David and all the Israelites marched to Jerusalem (that is, Jebus). The Jebusites who lived there said to David, "You will not get in here." Nevertheless, David captured the fortress of Zion, the City of David.* (1 Chron. 11:3–5 NIV)

Is the church facing the same situation today as David did, as we enter our third millennium? Are there not enemy strongholds in the high places of our nations that have seemingly been there forever? Not even the early church could drive them out. The Enemy is smug. "You will not get in here," he cries. "I have been entrenched in these high places for millennia; what makes you think you can dislodge me?"

The apostle Paul and the early church faced these same entrenched forces, and even they could not ultimately drive them out. How do we know this? Because they are still there.

> *For our struggle is not against flesh and blood, but against the rulers, against the authorities, against the powers of this dark world and against the spiritual forces of evil in the heavenly realms.* (Eph. 6:12 NIV)

To be sure, the New Testament church did win some resounding victories in their generation. None was greater than in Ephesus, where so many were converted to Christ that the city was in an uproar when the industries that had made money from idolatry began to fail:

> *A silversmith named Demetrius, who made silver shrines of Artemis [Diana], brought in no little business for the*

craftsmen. He called them together, along with the work-men in related trades, and said: "Men, you know we receive a good income from this business. And you see and hear how this fellow Paul has convinced and led astray large numbers of people....He says that man-made gods are no gods at all. There is danger not only that our trade will lose its good name, but also that the temple of the great goddess Artemis will be discredited."...When they heard this, they were furious. (Acts 19:24–28 NIV)

Many Christians today would be delighted to settle for these kinds of results. Although limited victories like this did occur in New Testament days, the firmly entrenched principalities and powers were never permanently removed. But there is a generation that will see these enemies driven out. It is no accident that the prophetic anointing of worship and warfare, which was first manifested in David's kingdom and propelled him to victory over all his enemies, is now returning to the church of Jesus Christ after three thousand years. Churches across the whole earth are prophesying new songs; acting out the Word of the Lord in physical movement; and rejoicing with great joy in dancing, shouting, clapping, and singing.

The Hebrew word *Jebusite* means a "threshing floor," a place that is "trodden down." The name comes from a Hebrew word meaning "to trample" or "to tread down underfoot." All during Israel's prior history, until the time of David, things had been upside down. The Enemy had been treading down the people of God. But when the Davidic era and anointing began, things turned right-side up. David's enemies were put under his feet. *"And the God of peace will crush Satan under your feet shortly"* (Rom. 16:20). *"These who have turned the world upside down have come here too"* (Acts 17:6). *"Behold, I give you the authority to trample on serpents and scorpions, and over all the power of the enemy, and nothing shall by any means hurt you"* (Luke 10:19).

A FRESH ANOINTING

The Davidic anointing is now bringing the same victory to the church as it did to Israel at its inception. The church is singing psalms again and is learning to worship the Father and rejoice in the Spirit with all the abandonment that was enjoyed in the days of David. David was lifted above all his enemies, and the surrounding nations were put under his feet. His kingdom was exalted as the highest power of his day. That same power of God released through prophetic worship and praise is now returning to the church of Jesus Christ in order to duplicate in every nation what happened in Zion three thousand years ago.

We are seeing in this generation a return to the most prevalent theme of the Psalms: a cry for the deliverance of the righteous from those who oppress and falsely accuse them.

In the tabernacle of David on Mount Zion, the throne of God ruled in power in an atmosphere of praise and worship:

> *In mercy the throne will be established; and One will sit on it in truth, in the tabernacle of David, judging and seeking justice and hastening righteousness.* (Isa. 16:5)

The kingdoms of David and Solomon represented the greatest reigns in Israel's history. All their enemies made peace with them and sent them tribute and gifts:

> *All King Solomon's drinking vessels were gold, and all the vessels of the House of the Forest of Lebanon were pure gold. Not one was silver, for this was accounted as nothing in the days of Solomon. For the king had merchant ships at sea with the fleet of Hiram. Once every three years the merchant ships came bringing gold, silver, ivory, apes, and monkeys. So King Solomon surpassed all the kings of the earth in riches and wisdom.* (1 Kings 10:21–23)

David won every battle he fought, and the Lord preserved him greatly:

> *When the Arameans [Syrians] of Damascus came to help Hadadezer king of Zobah, David struck down twenty-two thousand of them. He put garrisons in the Aramean kingdom of Damascus, and the Arameans became subject to him and brought tribute. The LORD gave David victory*

wherever he went....King David dedicated these articles to the LORD, as he had done with the silver and gold from all the nations he had subdued: Edom and Moab, the Ammonites and the Philistines, and Amalek....And David became famous after he returned from striking down eighteen thousand Edomites in the Valley of Salt. He put garrisons throughout Edom, and all the Edomites became subject to David. The LORD gave David victory wherever he went.

(2 Sam. 8:5-6, 11–14 NIV)

In like manner, at this point in the history of the church, the Son of David, the Lord Jesus Christ, is acting through His body, the church, to rule again with power in the earth by releasing through the church the Davidic anointing of prophetic worship and warfare. Mount Zion is again being established in all the nations as the highest power and authority in all the earth.

In the last days the mountain of the Lord's temple will be established as chief among the mountains; it will be raised above the hills, and all nations will stream to it.

(Isa. 2:2 NIV)

In Mount Zion, death itself will one day be ultimately destroyed, and all the nations of the earth will be set free from the bondage of corruption and decay. As in the days of David when his enemies were driven out of the high places where they had been entrenched for millennia, the stronghold of our ancient enemy will be brought down:

The hand of the LORD will rest on this mountain; but Moab will be trampled under him....He will bring down your high fortified walls and lay them low; he will bring them down to the ground, to the very dust.

(Isa. 25:10, 12 NIV)

In this mountain, Mount Zion, *"He will swallow up death forever"* (v. 8). *"He will bring down your high fortified walls and lay them low"* (v. 12 NIV) *"In mercy the throne will be established"* (Isa. 16:5). The glory of the Lord will be seen. Heaven will be displayed on earth. As this mountain grows and increases, it will gradually fill the whole earth with its influence, and all other kingdoms will be shattered:

> *And the stone that struck the image became a great mountain and filled the whole earth....And in the days of these kings the God of heaven will set up a kingdom which shall never be destroyed...it shall break in pieces and consume all these kingdoms, and it shall stand forever.*
>
> (Dan. 2:35, 44)

Chapter 18

The Final Kingdom

After the sin of Adam had cast a pall of death over the human race, heaven pulled away from the earth. Instead of the glory of God, animal skins now covered men (Gen. 3:21). No longer did they hear *"the sound of the LORD God walking in the garden in the cool of the day"* (v. 8), communing with men as before. A great separation set in between heaven and earth, between God and men. Satan, the *"god of this world"* (2 Cor. 4:4 KJV), was allowed to blind the minds of men: *"The god of this age has blinded the minds of unbelievers, so that they cannot see the light of the gospel of the glory of Christ"* (v. 4 NIV).

As the nations gradually spread out over the face of the earth, a shadowy covering was laid upon them. This veil of death was stretched out over all men: *"For in the day that you eat of it* [the tree of the knowledge of good and evil] *you shall surely die"* (Gen. 2:17). *"Therefore, just as sin entered the world through one man, and death through sin, and in this way death came to all men, because all sinned"* (Rom. 5:12 NIV).

Sin separated the whole human race from the Creator, and this separation between heaven and earth became firmly entrenched. Any bridging of this barrier would have to originate from above, in heaven. And it did, as is recorded numerous times in Scripture, such as when the glory of God came down from heaven and appeared to Moses on Mount Sinai, when the fire of God fell from heaven and consumed the sacrifices at Solomon's temple, when the angels appeared to the shepherds, or when the Holy Spirit was poured out in tongues of fire on the Day of Pentecost.

The ultimate invasion of heaven into the earth was, of course, the Incarnation of Jesus Christ, the only begotten Son of God. The actual image of God appeared again in human form, human life as it was originally meant to be, human life as it will one day fully become in Christ.

THE LEAVENING EFFECT

But the plan of God is not just limited to these vertical invasions of the powers of heaven into the earth, when Christ came or when the glory of God was revealed in a few isolated instances, nor will it be limited to snatching a few souls out of this world into heaven before the earth plunges into destruction. The plan of God has always included the progressive transformation of the earth and its people by the leavening effect of the kingdom of God through the ministry of the fully empowered church of Jesus Christ:

And again He said, "To what shall I liken the kingdom of God? It is like leaven, which a woman took and hid in three measures of meal till it was all leavened."
(Luke 13:20–21)

The kingdom of heaven is like yeast that a woman took and mixed into a large amount of flour until it worked all through the dough. (Matt. 13:33 NIV)

My prayer is not that you take them out of the world but that you protect them from the evil one....I pray also for those who will believe in me through their message....May they also be in us so that the world may believe that you have sent me. (John 17:15, 20–21 NIV)

For God did not send his Son into the world to condemn the world, but to save the world through him.
(John 3:17 NIV)

The intention of the God of Creation is to go far beyond occasionally piercing the darkness in human history for the purpose of populating heaven to actually removing the darkness itself from the earth and its people by ripping off the overshadowing veil of death from all nations:

> *And he will destroy in this mountain the face of the covering cast over all people, and the veil that is spread over all nations. He will swallow up death in victory.*
>
> (Isa. 25:7–8 KJV)

> *On this mountain he will destroy the shroud that enfolds all peoples, the sheet that covers all nations; he will swallow up death forever. The Sovereign LORD will wipe away the tears from all faces; he will remove the disgrace of his people from all the earth. The LORD has spoken.*
>
> (vv. 7–8 NIV)

What a vision for the culmination of the last days! If we are going to participate with the Lord in His momentous plan of the ages, we are going to have to grow in our faith and in our Holy Spirit anointing to a level above that of any other generation in church history, even beyond that of the New Testament church itself.

A GREATER GLORY

The Scriptures of both Testaments peer into the future to catch a glimpse of the glory of the Lord that will fill the earth by the end of the last days. The Word of the Lord teaches us that God always ends something with a greater glory than when it first began, and this certainly includes His church.

> *The end of a thing is better than its beginning.*   (Eccl. 7:8)

> *"The glory of this latter temple [church] shall be greater than the former," says the LORD of hosts. "And in this place I will give peace," says the LORD of hosts.*   (Hag. 2:9)

> *Christ also loved the church and gave Himself for her...that He might present her to Himself a glorious church, not having spot or wrinkle or any such thing, but that she should be holy and without blemish.*
>
> (Eph. 5:25, 27)

Now may the God of peace Himself sanctify you completely; and may your whole spirit, soul, and body be preserved blameless at the coming of our Lord Jesus Christ.

(1 Thess. 5:23)

We know that when He is revealed, we shall be like Him.

(1 John 3:2)

The church of Jesus Christ must be assured by the Word of God that as we enter into the third millennium of Christian history, a process of development and empowerment is beginning that will culminate in the radical transformation of the earth. *"The kingdoms of this world* [will] *become the kingdoms of our Lord and of His Christ"* (Rev. 11:15). The *"knowledge of the glory of the LORD"* will cover the earth as deeply as the *"waters cover the sea"* (Hab. 2:14). *"But truly, as I live, all the earth shall be filled with the glory of the LORD"* (Num. 14:21).

Think of it! The glory of the Lord will be a brand-new covering for the earth. Instead of being covered by the *"shadow of death"* (Ps. 23:4), spiritual darkness, and *"wickedness in high places"* (Eph. 6:12 KJV), the earth, at long last, will bask in the Sonlight of the glory of God. God's new Day will shine in all its brilliance. *"Then the righteous will shine forth as the sun in the kingdom of their Father"* (Matt. 13:43).

THE THIRD DAY

We are entering a transition between the end of two thousand years (two days) of Christian history and the beginning of the third millennium (the third day) of the church. Two thousand years is seemingly an endless time period, but it is only two days to God—two days since the last days began on the Day of Pentecost! *"And it shall come to pass in the last days, says God, that I will pour out of My Spirit on all flesh"* (Acts 2:17).

If the prophet Hosea was looking ahead to the church age (in 1 Peter 1:9–12, Peter taught that the Old Testament prophets were prophesying to the church), then his prophecy mentions a day of glorious life and resurrection power after two days (two thousand years?) of church history: *"After two days He will revive us; on the third day He will raise us up, that we may live in His sight"* (Hos. 6:2).

Are we entering this third day of the fullness of the glory of God when resurrection life will spring forth in the church? And is this third day also the seventh day of biblically recorded human history? Four thousand years of biblical history preceded the Cross of Calvary, going back to the existence of Adam and Eve. Was Christ crucified four days (four thousand years?) after biblical history began?

Interestingly, in the Jewish celebration of the Passover, the lamb was chosen the tenth day of the month, but wasn't sacrificed until four days later.

> *Tell the whole community of Israel that on the tenth day of this month each man is to take a lamb....Take care of them until the fourteenth day of the month, when all the people of the community of Israel must slaughter them at twilight.* (Exod. 12:3, 6 NIV)

So then, have there been four days (four thousand years) of biblical history prior to the Cross and two days (two thousand years) after the Cross to the present? Are these last two days of church history actually the fifth and sixth days of biblical history? Is the third day of the church actually the seventh day of biblical history and also the final and glorious Day of the Lord that all the prophets foretold? *"And I saw thrones, and they sat on them, and judgment was committed to them....And they lived and reigned with Christ for a thousand years* [the seventh day?]*"*(Rev. 20:4).

A SABBATH REST

The New Testament declares that there is a generation of the people of God who will enter into God's seventh day of Sabbath rest, when God's people will cease from their own labors in order to enter into the full work of God:

> *For we who have believed do enter that rest....For He has spoken...of the seventh day* [a period of a thousand years?]

Experiencing God's Power in Worship

..."And God rested on the seventh day from all His works."...There remains therefore a rest for the people of God. For he who has entered His rest has himself also ceased from his works as God did from His. Let us therefore be diligent to enter that rest. (Heb. 4:3–4, 9–11)

As God rested from his own work on the seventh day, we are to enter a period of time when the church will rest from its own labor and self-effort in order to enter a period of divine rest, by experiencing a Spirit-led and Spirit-empowered life and ministry beyond that of any other generation. For God's seventh day rest involves doing the works of the Spirit.

Jesus corrected the false concepts of the Pharisees, who understood the meaning of Sabbath rest as the absence of work and who criticized Jesus for working on the Sabbath by healing a man:

Because Jesus was doing these things on the Sabbath, the Jews persecuted Him. Jesus said to them, "My Father is always at his work to this very day, and I, too, am working."..."The Son can do nothing by himself; he can only do what he sees his Father doing, because whatever the Father does the Son also does. For the Father loves the Son and shows him all he does. Yes, to your amazement he will show him even greater things than these."
(John 5:16–17, 19–20 NIV)

What a glorious prospect for our future! Imagine being able to cease from our human efforts and rise in the Spirit's power into a new fullness of the miracle-working Spirit of God. In the fullness of the Spirit, the church will actually do the works of the Father that Jesus did!

We already know what this is like to a certain extent, for the Spirit-filled believer has received a measure of the Spirit's gifts and ministries. From time to time, we see with prophetic eyes what God sees, say what He is saying, and do the miraculous works that God is doing. But imagine moving more permanently into such a realm of living and entering into the Sabbath rest of God Himself!

TRANSFORMED IN HIS IMAGE

We have a glorious, transforming metamorphosis to look forward to as the church of Jesus Christ, appearing to the scoffers of this world as a lowly caterpillar, suddenly takes wings and as a beautiful butterfly, soars into the heavens. Is this wonderful transformation reserved for the millennium we are now entering? Are we now making the transition into the third day of church history and the seventh day of biblically recorded human history?

Has God not given us in Christ, who is His glorious image, the perfect representation of God the Father and also the image of a perfectly restored humanity? Did not God at the very inception of Creation give us a preview of the glory to come, which will ultimately fill our lives? For by the end of the sixth day, mankind had emerged into the full image of God Himself. Does this foretell that after six days of biblical history (six thousand years), redeemed and recreated man—the church—will again emerge in the full image of God?

> *Then God said, "Let Us make man in Our image, according to Our likeness; let them have dominion."...So God created man in His own image; in the image of God He created him....Then God blessed them, and God said to them, "Be fruitful and multiply; fill the earth and subdue it."...So the evening and the morning were the sixth day.*
>
> (Gen. 1:26–28, 31)

Did our Lord give us a preview in His own transfiguration of the glory of God that would transform the church *"after six days* [or six thousand years of biblical history]*"* (Mark 9:2)? For it was *"after six days"* that Jesus was transfigured before His disciples; the full glory of the kingdom of God shone from Him:

> *And he said to them, "I tell you the truth, some who are standing here will not taste death before they see the kingdom of God come with power."* (Mark 9:1 NIV)

> *After six days Jesus took Peter, James and John with him and led them up a high mountain....There he was transfigured before them.* (Mark 9:2 NIV)

As the seventh day of Creation began (the kingdom Age?) there was a man (the body of Christ?) fully representing the image of God and ready to rule and reign over the earth. *"Then God said, 'Let us make man in our image, in our likeness, and let them rule over the fish of the sea and the birds of the air, over the livestock, over all the earth'"* (Gen. 1:26 NIV). God could afford to rest on the seventh day because He could entrust the earth into the care of man, who was fully formed in His image.

As the church is now entering the seventh day of biblical history (the seventh period of one thousand years), are we now to fulfill the preview of human history given to us at the beginning of Creation? Does God want to perfect or mature the church to reflect the full image of God, as Christ is formed in us, so that we may cease from our self-efforts and enter into the Sabbath rest (the seventh day) of God's kingdom?

What a wonderful divine exchange! God rests from His own work, and we rest from our work and enter into His. As a proud Father, He can now sit back and enjoy seeing His children run the business. For Adam's original job was to rule and reign over the beasts (kingdoms?) of the earth. Man was to *"have dominion over...every living thing"* (Gen. 1:28).

FAITH TO REIGN

The Christian church has never taken seriously its mandate to rule and reign over the whole earth and to subdue it. This concept seems so far beyond us, so remote, so unobtainable. We wistfully look ahead in our imagination to a time in the distant future when Christ will return as King and do it all. But now we feel stuck in our own generational muck and mire and are trying to make the best of mere spiritual survival in the midst of an increasingly godless age. What we need is a truly biblical faith:

> *Who through faith conquered kingdoms, administered justice, and gained what was promised; who shut the mouths of lions, quenched the fury of the flames, and escaped the edge of the sword; whose weakness was turned to strength; and who became powerful in battle and routed foreign armies.* (Heb. 11:33–34 NIV)

The Final Kingdom

We need the faith of David, who, when faced with Goliath's challenge, was not limited to merely defeating the giant, but saw in the Spirit the ultimate defeat of the entire Philistine army:

> David said to the Philistine, "You come against me with sword and spear and javelin, but I come against you in the name of the LORD Almighty, the God of the armies of Israel, whom you have defied. This day the LORD will hand you over to me, and I'll strike you down and cut off your head. Today I will give the carcasses of the Philistine army to the birds of the air and the beasts of the earth, and the whole world will know that there is a God in Israel."
>
> (1 Sam. 17:45–46 NIV)

Is this same trumpet of victorious faith sounding in our own day? Is it time for us to rise up in faith to defeat the enemies of the kingdom of God and inherit the promises given to the saints? We dare not be caught with our heads stuck in the sand, unaware of the cosmic, eternal plan of God that is now unfolding for the church as it enters its third millennium.

Chapter 19

Faith or Fear?

Faith involves expectation. If we believe something will happen, we expect it to happen. Our theology, or our system of belief, about the last days determines what we expect to happen in the future. Christians looking toward the future have radically different expectations. Some have fears of doom and gloom, while others hope for kingdom victory. Some churches terrify their congregations with expectations of torturous times of tribulation, while others excite their people with hopes of a universal, glorious kingdom reign.

Both sides use Scripture. Both sides are in Scripture. Jesus taught us that *"the harvest is the end of the age"* (Matt. 13:39). As we approach the harvest, there are two crops that are ripening, or maturing: the tares, *"the sons of the wicked one,"* and the wheat, *"the sons of the kingdom"* (v. 38). Both plants *"grow [up] together until the harvest"* (v. 30). Positive and negative coexist. Things are going to get worse and worse in the world and better and better in the church.

IN GOOD TIMES AND BAD

What is our expectation to be as we approach the end of this age? Will the church be gripped with fear or girded with faith? We can find help in answering these questions by looking at the end of the Old Testament age. God has already closed out that biblical era, and quite possibly, He has left some signposts there that point to the end of our own church age: *"These things happened to them as examples and were written down for us, on whom the fulfillment of the ages has come"* (1 Cor. 10:11 NIV).

The end of the New Testament age may be very similar to the end of the Old Testament era: terrible times of persecution were followed by glorious revival, which swept whole empires into the influence of the kingdom of God. It was both a positive and a negative time.

Imagine living in the days of the Old Testament and approaching the *"time of the end"* (Dan. 12:4). These were fearful and foreboding times. Cities were destroyed by pagan armies, people were taken captive by other nations, furnaces of fire were prepared for worshipers of God, laws against prayer included dens of lions awaiting the lawbreakers, and death sentences were pronounced against the people of God. It was horrible!

Yet as we study that history more carefully, an incredibly glorious picture also emerges. God was wonderfully with His people during those terrible times. He not only saved every one of them out of their tribulations, but also used their mighty deliverances to turn nations, even whole empires, to Him.

These stories of deliverance are well-known even to Sunday school children, but we as adults rarely take them seriously. We never read beyond these individual rescues to realize the ultimate purpose of God in accomplishing them.

THE BAD NEWS

What about the three Hebrew children: Hananiah, Mishael, and Azariah? We know them better by their Chaldean names: Shadrach, Meschah, and Abednego. They were told, *"Whoever does not fall down and worship* [the Babylonian kingdom personified by the golden statue of Nebuchadnezzar] *will immediately be thrown into a blazing furnace"* (Dan. 3:6 NIV). We know the story well, but do we take it seriously?

Daniel faced a similar persecution when an edict went out in all the empire of the Persians that prohibited prayer to any god. Daniel faithfully disobeyed this order and even continued his public prayer by opening his windows toward Jerusalem and praying three times a day, as usual. (See Daniel 6:10.)

Even worse was the death sentence passed upon all the people of God in the days of Esther. A decree was issued that on the thirteenth day of the twelfth month of that year, all Jews would be put to death. Their enemies were allowed by law *"to destroy, to kill, and to cause to perish, all Jews, both young and old, little children and women, in one day"* (Est. 3:13 KJV).

THE REST OF THE STORY

What awful times in which to live! What terrible persecution! Who would ever want to experience such times? But wait! We must read the rest of the story. The amazing truth is that all these people were totally and miraculously delivered from their persecutions: the three Hebrew children, Daniel, Esther and all her people. Everyone escaped death! Even more amazing is the fact that empire-wide changes of spiritual climate occurred each time, as a result of these deliverances.

SAVED FROM FIRE

Every Bible student knows the three Hebrew children were miraculously delivered from the fiery furnace, a furnace so hot that *"the flames of the fire killed the soldiers who took up Shadrach, Meshach and Abednego"* (Dan. 3:22 NIV). But the final result of this miracle, an evangelistic impact upon the whole empire, is even more amazing:

> *Then Nebuchanezzar said, "Praise be to the God of Shadrach, Meschah and Abednego, who has sent his angel and rescued his servants! They trusted in him and defied the king's command and were willing to give up their lives rather than serve or worship any god except their own God. Therefore I decree that the people of any nation or language who say anything against the God of Shadrach, Meschah and Abednego be cut into pieces...for no other god can save in this way."* (Dan. 3:28–29 NIV)

DELIVERED FROM LIONS

When Daniel was delivered from the lions, it sparked a worldwide revival:

> *Then King Darius wrote: To all peoples, nations, and lan-*
> *guages that dwell in all the earth....I make a decree that in*
> *every dominion of my kingdom men must tremble and fear*
> *before the God of Daniel. For He is the living God...and*
> *His kingdom is the one which shall not be destroyed, and*
> *His dominion shall endure to the end. He delivers and res-*
> *cues, and He works signs and wonders in heaven and on*
> *earth.* (Dan. 6:25–27)

Not only was Daniel honored, but all the men who had accused him, including their families, were themselves thrown to the lions: *"They brought those men who had accused Daniel, and they cast them into the den of lions; them, their children, and their wives"* (v. 24).

Imagine such a turnaround! It was such a political about-face that the world rulers began persecuting the enemies of the people of God. Nebuchadnezzar and Darius actually commanded their world empires to worship and honor the true God and His servants. Do we need this same kind of faith and expectancy in our generation?

All it took to remove the influence of the principalities and powers that were arrayed against the people of God was for the earthly kings to simply change their minds and turn from fighting against the Lord and His people to honoring and lifting them up. At that moment, the demonic strongholds over those nations lost all their influence, for the human authorities changed from serving them to honoring Jehovah. It was simple! In a moment, they lost their foothold, their human channels, and therefore, their influence.

THE JEWS SAVED FROM DESTRUCTION

In Esther's day, there was such a turnaround in the planned extermination of the Jews, that not only did all the Jews survive, but many other people of the empire also converted to become people of God:

> *Now in the twelfth month...on the thirteenth day, the time*
> *came for the king's command and his decree to be exe-*
> *cuted. On the day that the enemies of the Jews had hoped*

to overpower them, the opposite occurred, in that the Jews themselves overpowered those who hated them. The Jews gathered together...to lay hands on those who sought their harm. And no one could withstand them, because fear of them fell upon all people....And Mordecai wrote...to establish among them that they should celebrate yearly the fourteenth and the fifteenth days of the month of Adar, as the days on which the Jews had rest from their enemies, as the month which was turned from sorrow to joy for them, and from mourning to a holiday....The Jews had light and gladness, joy and honor....Then many of the people of the land became Jews, because fear of the Jews fell upon them.
(Est. 9:1–2, 20–22; 8:16–17)

Not only did the Jews have complete victory over all their enemies, but also their accuser, Haman, (a type of Satan) was put to death by being hung on his own gallows:

Look! The gallows, fifty cubits high, which Haman made for Mordecai....Then the king said, "Hang him on it!" So they hanged Haman on the gallows that he had prepared for Mordecai.
(Est. 7:9–10)

BAD TURNED TO GOOD

What a turnaround occurred at the end of the Old Testament age! What started so negatively—with fiery furnaces, lions' dens, laws against prayer, and death sentences—actually ended up so positively that whole empires were turned to the Lord. One phrase in the book of Esther describes this 180-degree turn from negative to positive: *"though it was turned to the contrary"* (Est. 9:1 KJV).

This is the message trumpeted loud and clear from the end times of the Old Testament: the tribulation and persecution of the people of God was *"turned to the contrary"*!

Is God showing us in the end of the Old Testament age a preview of our own last days? Is the history of the end of the Old Testament age an illustration of the end of the church age? The New Testament teaches that *"these things [in Old Testament history] happened to them as examples and were written down as*

warnings for us, on whom the fulfillment of the ages has come"
(1 Cor. 10:11 NIV).

Could it be that such incredible deliverances await the
church of Jesus Christ in our own day? Could it be that God
could turn Satan's attempts to snuff out the church in our generation *"to the contrary"*? Can we believe for the complete turnaround of foreign nations now hostile to the church? Can we
have this world-turning faith today?

It is awesome to realize what God has already done once in
history. He actually caused pagan leaders to totally reverse their
position toward His people, so that they not only stopped persecuting them but also helped them accomplish their mission and
promoted them:

> *Then the king promoted Shadrach, Meshach, and Abed-*
> *nego in the province of Babylon.*　　　　(Dan. 3:30)

> *So this Daniel prospered in the reign of Darius and in the*
> *reign of Cyrus the Persian.*　　　　(Dan. 6:28)

> *For Mordecai the Jew was second to King Ahasuerus, and*
> *was great among the Jews...seeking the good of his people*
> *and speaking peace to all his countrymen.*　　　(Est. 10:3)

This is consistent with other "last day" examples at the end
of Old Testament history, when pagan world governments, after
they mercilessly persecuted the people of God, actually ended up
favoring them, by providing them tax deductions and financial
and material aid. These governments had learned that their
earthly reigns were blessed by the people of God and their worship of Jehovah:

> *Moreover I issue a decree as to what you shall do for the*
> *elders of these Jews, for the building of this house of God:*
> *Let the cost be paid at the king's expense from taxes on the*
> *region beyond the River; this is to be given immediately to*
> *these men, so that they are not hindered. And whatever*
> *they need; young bulls, rams, and lambs for the burnt of-*
> *ferings of the God of heaven, wheat, salt, wine, and oil,*

according to the request of the priests who are in Jerusalem; let it be given them day by day without fail, that they may offer sacrifices of sweet aroma to the God of heaven, and pray for the life of the king and his sons. Also I issue a decree that whoever alters this edict, let a timber be pulled from his house and erected, and let him be hanged on it; and let his house be made a refuse heap because of this.

(Ezra 6:8–11)

You are to carry the silver and gold which the king and his counselors have freely offered to the God of Israel, whose dwelling is in Jerusalem....And whatever seems good to you and your brethren to do with the rest of the silver and the gold, do it according to the will of your God....And whatever more may be needed for the house of your God,... pay for it from the king's treasury....Whatever is commanded by the God of heaven, let it diligently be done for the house of the God of heaven. For why should there be wrath against the realm of the king and his sons? Also we inform you that it shall not be lawful to impose tax, tribute, or custom on any of the priests, Levites, singers, gatekeepers, Nethinim, or servants of this house of God....Whoever will not observe the law of your God and the law of the king, let judgment be executed speedily on him, whether it be death, or banishment, or confiscation of goods, or imprisonment. (Ezra 7:15, 18, 20, 23–24, 26)

FAITH THAT OVERCOMES

The kind of faith needed for our own end time is the kind of faith that believes God and does not fear anyone but the Lord. It is the kind of faith mentioned in Hebrews 11, when the faith heroes of Scripture are listed:

Who through faith subdued kingdoms, worked righteousness, obtained promises, stopped the mouths of lions, quenched the violence of fire, escaped the edge of the sword, out of weakness were made strong,...turned to flight the armies of the aliens. (Heb. 11:33–34)

We need to fortify our churches in these last days with this kind of overcoming faith, so that we can be ready when it is time for the *"kingdoms of this world* [to] *become the kingdoms of our Lord and of His Christ"* (Rev. 11:15).

> *This is the victory that has overcome the world, even our faith.* (1 John 5:4 NIV)

Chapter 20

The Glory of the Last-Day Church

The apostle Paul declared that *"the ends of the ages have come"* (1 Cor. 10:11) upon the church of Jesus Christ. The church is entering its third millennium with the help of a scriptural record that has already documented the conclusion of one biblical era, the Old Testament age. God apparently orchestrated Old Testament history to preview that of the church.

When the prophet Haggai declared at the end of the Old Testament age, *"The glory of this latter house shall be greater than of the former"* (Hag. 2:9 KJV), he may have thought he was prophesying about the temple built in his day, after the exile in Babylon. We know that the dimensions of this temple were bigger than Solomon's, by comparing 1 Kings 6:2 with Ezra 6:3, where the height of the *"latter"* house was twice that of the *"former,"* and its width was three times as large.

But did Haggai know the full extent of what he was saying by the Spirit? Was God also declaring prophetically that we are to expect the glory of the "latter" church to exceed that of "former" church of New Testament days? Certainly the New Testament teaches us that Old Testament prophets were not ultimately ministering to their own people in their own day when they prophesied, but they were speaking to us, the church:

> *The prophets have inquired and searched carefully, who prophesied of the grace that would come to you, searching what, or what manner of time, the Spirit of Christ who was in them was indicating when He testified beforehand the sufferings of Christ and the glories that would follow.*

> *To them it was revealed that, not to themselves, but to us*
> [the Church] *they were ministering.*   (1 Pet. 1:10–12)

Throughout the Old Testament, there are many illustrations of the glory of the Last-Day church. In fact, the Word of God summarizes the purposes of God in all of history when it simply declares: *"The end of a thing is better than its beginning"* (Eccl. 7:8).

Has the Lord given us a preview of the history of the church in the book of Job? It appears so. Job began his life with great natural wealth and blessings, as did the early church with great spiritual blessings:

> *There was a man in the land of Uz, whose name was Job....His possessions were seven thousand sheep, three thousand camels, five hundred yoke of oxen, five hundred female donkeys, and a very large household, so that this man was the greatest of all the people of the East.*
> (Job 1:1, 3)

After this glorious beginning, he entered a time of great testing, trials, and deprivation, analogous to what the church of Jesus Christ has experienced throughout most of its history. Yet the end of Job's life was tremendously blessed, hopefully foreshadowing a wonderful blessing at the end of the church age. He received twice what he had before:

> *The LORD restored Job's losses when he prayed for his friends. Indeed the LORD gave Job twice as much as he had before....Now the LORD blessed the latter days of Job more than his beginning; for he had fourteen thousand sheep, six thousand camels, one thousand yoke of oxen, and one thousand female donkeys.*   (Job 42:10, 12)

The prophet Elisha apparently shocked his predecessor, when he asked for twice the anointing and power of the Holy Spirit that Elijah had:

> *Elijah said to Elisha, "Ask! What may I do for you, before I am taken away from you?" Elisha said, "Please let a*

*double portion of your spirit be upon me." So he said, "You
have asked a hard thing."* (2 Kings 2:9–10)

Elisha did receive a double portion of the Holy Spirit, with
not only more miracles, but more powerful ones, than those of
Elijah. As a possible preview of the last days, Elijah represents a
prophetic ministry that was retired to heaven in a chariot of
fire, while Elisha carried on a powerful ministry of the kingdom
of God in the earth with twice the impact!

Was the prophet Isaiah looking down the corridor of time to
see the future glory of the last-day church when he prophesied:

> *But you shall be named the priests of the LORD, they shall
> call you the servants of our God. You shall eat the riches of
> the Gentiles, and in their glory you shall boast. Instead of
> your shame you shall have double honor, and instead of
> confusion they shall rejoice in their portion. Therefore in
> their land they shall possess double.* (Isa. 61:6–7)

The patriarch Jacob, like Job, can also serve as an example
of the glory of the church of Jesus Christ in the last days. After
twenty years of much testing and proving in Haran, Jacob returned at the end of his life to the land of Canaan with such
great wealth that his possessions eclipsed those of his brother,
Esau:

> *Thus the man became exceedingly prosperous, and had
> large flocks, female and male servants, and camels and
> donkeys....For all these riches which God has taken from
> our father are really ours....And he carried away all his
> livestock and all his possessions which he had gained...to
> go to his father Isaac in the land of Canaan.*
> (Gen. 30:43; 31:16, 18)

The nation of Israel may also be seen as a parable of the
church. At its inception, Israel came out of Egypt by a great deliverance with much wealth and blessing, even as the church
has been saved out of the world by a wonderful deliverance:

> *Now the children of Israel...had asked from the Egyptians
> articles of silver, articles of gold, and clothing. And the*

LORD had given the people favor in the sight of the Egyptians, so that they granted them what they requested. Thus they plundered the Egyptians. (Exod. 12:35–36)

After leaving Egypt, much like the church, Israel experienced an extended period of testing, trials, and wandering in the desert. However, in the glorious conclusion of their wilderness journey, they experienced complete victory over all the nations of the promised land and fully inherited all their promised possessions. Is not this to be the future of the church as well? Are we not to believe for *"the kingdoms of this world"* to *"become the kingdoms of our Lord and of His Christ"* (Rev. 11:15)?

The Old Testament abounds with prophetic illustrations concerning the glory of God upon the church of Jesus Christ in the last days. The New Testament confirms this, as it envisions the Bridegroom presenting to Himself a wonderful bride, *"a glorious church, not having spot or wrinkle or any such thing, but that she should be holy and without blemish"* (Eph. 5:27).

The apostle Paul prayed that by the time of the coming of the Lord, the church would be completely sanctified, with a *"blameless"* spirit, soul, and body (1 Thess. 5:23).

The apostle Peter urged the church to be diligent, so that at His coming, we may be *"found by Him in peace, without spot and blameless"* (2 Pet. 3:14).

The apostle John declared that by the time Christ appears, the church will have matured in character to actually be like Him!

We know that when He is revealed, we shall be like Him, for we shall see Him as He is. And everyone who has this hope in Him purifies himself, just as He is pure. (1 John 3:2–3)

The most awesome declaration of the state of the church at the conclusion of its development is found in Ephesians. In this epistle, the church is seen to mature under the ministries of the apostle, prophet, evangelist, pastor, and teacher, until we actually experience the fullness of Christ!

The Glory of the Last-Day Church

And He Himself gave some to be apostles, some prophets, some evangelists, and some pastors and teachers, for the equipping of the saints for the work of ministry, for the edifying of the body of Christ, till we all come to the unity of the faith and of the knowledge of the Son of God, to a perfect man, to the measure of the stature of the fullness of Christ. (Eph. 4:11–13)

This is a marvelous goal to believe for: obtaining the fullness of Christ Himself! The apostle Paul declared that the church *"is His body, the fullness of Him who fills all in all"* (Eph. 1:23).

If this is true, then the New Testament in its prophetic vision sees the church going beyond a mere double portion of the Holy Spirit in the end times to actually experiencing a limitless outpouring of God's power and anointing! Like her Lord, who had the Spirit poured through Him without measure, the church is to have a limitless supply for the last days:

For he whom God hath sent speaketh the words of God: for God giveth not the Spirit by measure unto him.
(John 3:34 KJV)

And of his fulness have all we received, and grace for grace. (John 1:16 KJV)

We have an encouraging prospect for our future, a limitless supply of the grace of God. It will certainly take this fullness of grace to help provide the church with the kind of faith it will need at the culmination of its present history. We need this kind of faith to believe that the kingdom of God will actually fill all the earth and that *"the earth will be filled with the knowledge of the glory of the LORD, as the waters cover the sea"* (Hab. 2:14).

Chapter 21

A Universal Kingdom

The prophet Daniel declared that certain prophecies of Scripture were *"sealed till the time of the end"* (Dan. 12:9). In one of his greatest insights, he saw the kingdom of God filling the whole earth. The Lord showed this to Daniel in the form of a vision, as He laid out for him the progression of world empires that would last until the time of Christ:

> *You, O king, were watching; and behold, a great image! This great image...was awesome. This image's head was of fine gold* [Babylonians], *its chest and arms of silver* [Medes and Persians], *its belly and thighs of bronze* [Greeks], *its legs of iron, its feet partly of clay* [Romans]. *You watched while a stone was cut out without hands, which struck the image on its feet of iron and clay, and broke them in pieces. Then the iron, the clay, the bronze, the silver, and the gold were crushed together, and became like chaff from the summer threshing floors; the wind carried them away so that no trace of them was found. And the stone that struck the image became a great mountain and filled the whole earth.* (Dan. 2:31–35)

What is this stone cut out of the mountain, which ultimately destroyed all previous kingdoms on earth and took their place? It is the kingdom of God.

> *And in the days of these kings* [a weakened Roman Empire, typified by iron mixed with clay] *the God of heaven will set up a kingdom which shall never be destroyed; and*

> *the kingdom shall...break in pieces and consume all these*
> *kingdoms, and it shall stand forever.* (Dan. 2:44)

THE UNSEEN KINGDOM

The kingdom of God is a great mountain, destined to rule over and fill the whole earth. What is this mountain? We are told that we, the church of Jesus Christ, *"have come to Mount Zion"* (Heb. 12:22). This mountain is the kingdom of God, that unseen kingdom cut out without human hands that was first manifest in the reign of David. This is the mountain of Zion from which King David reigned over all his enemies and over all the kingdoms of his day and upon which he established his prophetic priesthood of worship and praise in the tabernacle of David:

> *In mercy the throne will be established; and One will sit on*
> *it in truth, in the tabernacle of David, judging and seeking*
> *justice and hastening righteousness.* (Isa. 16:5)

This mountain receded from the earth in the centuries following King David, but the *"stone...cut out of the mountain"* (Dan. 2:45) came back into the earth when Jesus Christ was incarnated as the Son of David.

THE CHIEF CORNERSTONE

After His resurrection and ascension to the right hand of the Father, Jesus Christ assumed the throne of David, and the kingdom of God began to grow again in the earth, just as Daniel had seen in his vision:

> *Therefore, being a prophet* [David], *and knowing that God*
> *had sworn with an oath to him that of the fruit of his body,*
> *according to the flesh, He would raise up the Christ to sit*
> *on his throne, he, foreseeing this, spoke concerning the*
> *resurrection of the Christ.* (Acts 2:30–31)

The stone was cut out of the mountain. The mountain of God's eternal, heavenly kingdom once filled the earth with its power and authority in the reign of David, who ruled over all the nations around him. This kingdom came back to the earth again in Christ, the Chief Cornerstone, which was laid in Zion: *"See, I lay a stone in Zion, a chosen and precious cornerstone, and the one who trusts in him will never be put to shame"* (1 Pet. 2:6 NIV).

From the days of the early church, this stone has been growing, as the kingdom of God is now permeating the nations of the earth through the empowered church of Jesus Christ. It is destined to continue to increase in our own day, until ultimately, according to Daniel's vision, it becomes a mountain that fills *"the whole earth"* (Dan. 2:35).

AN EXALTED KINGDOM

This Mount Zion, to which we have come as Christians, this mountain of the kingdom of God, is to be exalted in the last days above all other authority and power on earth:

Now it shall come to pass in the latter days that the mountain of the Lord's house shall be established on the top of the mountains, and shall be exalted above the hills; and all nations shall flow to it. (Isa. 2:2)

In this mountain The LORD...will make for all people a feast. (Isa. 25:6)

And He will destroy on this mountain the surface of the covering cast over all people. (v. 7)

He will swallow up death in victory. (v. 8 KJV)

"For on this mountain the hand of the Lord will rest...[as the enemies of the people of God] *shall be trampled down under Him."* (v. 10)

The fortress of the high fort...He will bring down [the destruction of principalities and powers]. (v. 12)

In the church of Jesus Christ, we have all come to this mountain. The book of Hebrews teaches that this Mount Zion is really a heavenly place, which is now the equivalent of the Spirit-filled church:

> *But you have come to Mount Zion and to the city of the living God, the heavenly Jerusalem, to an innumerable company of angels, to the general assembly and church of the firstborn who are registered in heaven.* (Heb. 12:22–23)

A PLACE TO WORSHIP

Jesus told the woman at Jacob's well that any place on earth where God was worshiped *"in spirit and truth"* (John 4:23) would become an expression of the mountain of true worship, *"Mount Zion"* (Heb. 12:22):

> *Believe me, woman, a time is coming when you will worship the Father neither on this mountain* [the Samaritan mountain of worship] *nor in Jerusalem* [the Jewish mountain of worship]....*A time is coming and has now come when the true worshipers will worship the Father in spirit and truth.* (John 4:21, 23 NIV)

Mount Zion is the place of true spirit-filled worship of the Father. It is manifested wherever true worship is expressed. Isaiah saw this Mount Zion covered with assemblies of worshipers, and these assemblies were themselves covered with the glory of God. What wonderful descriptions he gave of this covering of protection over the churches! It was a *"glory"* (Isa. 4:5 NIV), a *"canopy"* (v. 5 NIV), a *"tabernacle"* (v. 6), a *"shelter"* (v. 6 NIV), a *"refuge"* (v. 6 NIV), a *"hiding place"* (v. 6 NIV), a *"covert"* (v. 6 KJV), a *"cloud of smoke"* (v. 5 NIV), a *"flaming fire"* (v. 5), a *"shade"* (v. 6 NIV), and a *"shadow"* (v. 6 KJV).

> *Then the LORD will create over all of Mount Zion and over those who assemble there a cloud of smoke by day and a glow of flaming fire by night; over all the glory will be a canopy. It will be a shelter and shade from the heat of the day, and a refuge and hiding place from the storm and rain.* (vv. 5–6 NIV)

A Universal Kingdom

THE CHURCH IN WORSHIP AND WORSHIP IN THE CHURCH

Another dual manifestation of the reality of blending heaven and earth in true worship is seen in the assemblies on Mount Zion and Mount Zion in the assemblies. In one sense, the local assemblies are seen to be on Mount Zion, but in another sense, Mount Zion is being expressed in the assemblies, as God establishes beachheads of His glory in His church throughout all nations. The canopy of spiritual darkness and death that has covered the earth since Adam is being invaded by the light of the glory of the Lord. Expressions of that light are now found everywhere on earth, for Christian believers everywhere have been called *"out of darkness into His marvelous light"* (1 Pet. 2:9) and have been delivered *"from the power of darkness and conveyed...into the kingdom of the Son of His love"* (Col. 1:13).

A TASTE OF WHAT IS COMING

These heavenly invasions of divine light and glory, which have pierced earth's atmosphere of spiritual darkness, are the foretaste of the ultimate victory that will one day universally cover the earth. The whole creation is predestined to be set free from the corruption produced by sin. The earth will be released from decay and death and will experience the same kind of liberty now enjoyed by the church in the realms of the Spirit. What is being experienced today in Spirit-filled worship and the manifested glory of God is to be extended over the whole world. The church in its third millennium must believe what the apostle Paul taught:

> *I consider that our present sufferings are not worth comparing with the glory that will be revealed in us....We know that the whole creation has been groaning as in the pains of childbirth right up to the present time....We wait eagerly for our adoption as sons, the redemption of our bodies.* (Rom. 8:18, 22–23 NIV)

A universal, worldwide reign, with the kingdom of God ruling the whole earth, was a primary vision of the New Testament church: "We have begun to experience now the glory of the Lord, which will one day cover the entire world. We, the Spirit-filled church, have tasted the goodness of the Word of God and the powers of the coming age" (Heb. 6:5, author's paraphrase).

They knew they had experienced foretastes of the kingdom that would ultimately supersede all other earthly powers. This kingdom of light is beginning to spread across the earth with ever increasing speed, as the church of Jesus Christ becomes stronger and stronger and threatens more powerfully the very authority of the *"prince of the power of the air"* (Eph. 2:2). One day, the church will rise to meet her Lord *"in the air"* (1 Thess. 4:17), the previous realm of the operation of principalities and powers, and fully expel Satan's influence from the earth!

Chapter 22

Your Kingdom Come

This coming kingdom made its first appearance in the life and reign of King David. It first appeared on geographical Mount Zion, the fortress captured by King David, which was turned into the first place on earth where an actual priesthood of worshipers was established. It was on Mount Zion that David constructed his new tabernacle, which housed the ark of the covenant, before which the priests ministered to the Lord in song and expressive worship. Through the worshipers, the Holy Spirit prophesied and was visibly manifested in their movements of praise and worship. It was in this tabernacle of David on Mount Zion that worshipers lifted their hands in adoration, clapped for joy, danced with exuberance, shouted with excitement, bowed in reverence, prophesied new songs, and played all manner of musical instruments to the Lord.

Over two hundred years after the death of David, the prophet Amos declared that this worship born on Mount Zion would again appear in the last days: *"On that day I will raise up the tabernacle of David, which has fallen down, and repair its damages; I will raise up its ruins, and rebuild it as in the days of old"* (Amos 9:11).

The apostle James declared that the church was the fulfillment of this prophecy of Amos and therefore was actually the restored tabernacle of David on spiritual Mount Zion, the city to which all believers have now come in the Spirit. James declared that the New Testament church was the fulfillment of the ancient prophecy of Amos, over seven hundred years earlier:

> *Simon [Peter] has declared how God at the first visited the Gentiles to take out of them a people for His name. And*

Experiencing God's Power in Worship

with this the words of the prophets agree, just as it is writ-
ten: "After this I will return and will rebuild the taberna-
cle of David, which has fallen down; I will build its ruins,
and I will set it up; so that the rest of mankind may seek
the LORD, even all the Gentiles who are called by My name,
says the LORD."   (Acts 15:14–17)

THE ZION PRINCIPLE

Since the days of the New Testament church, this Zion principle of true prophetic worship has been spreading across the whole earth. God has established Zion's mountain peaks everywhere, opening holes in the spiritual darkness to let the light of the kingdom of heaven shine down—penetrating and pushing back the darkness, as the church, which is the gateway into the heavenlies, rises in greater and greater displays of God's glory. These expressions of the kingdom of God are being universally manifested through Spirit-filled assemblies on Mount Zion. These churches are experiencing a foretaste, a preview, a down payment of that glory of God that will one day cover the whole earth and link the body of Christ in all nations. As Spirit-filled churches are proliferating in all the world, the light source of each local church is now being linked as if by fiber optics with all other light sources. The canopy of divine light and glory is increasing and spreading across the face of the whole earth.

We are now living under the covering of God's presence, manifested in and displayed through the church of Jesus Christ. We are experiencing His wonderful kingdom before it ultimately reigns over the whole world, after the darkness of the satanic atmosphere of evil ruling powers has been expelled. *"The gods that have not made the heavens and the earth shall perish from the earth and from under these heavens"* (Jer. 10:11).

CLAIM THE VICTORY

What a challenge for the church today to already be living in the kingdom that will one day rule all nations! As we reach the end of two thousand years of the church age, we are standing on the threshold of the greatest transformation in all of human history. We are in for something unprecedented. It is BIG. Let us give up our siege mentality, our ghetto complex, whereby we see ourselves as the despised few, waiting to be rescued from the earth before it plunges into destruction. On the contrary, the Lord is challenging us to have the faith of Joshua and David, who conquered enemy territory that no other former generation had been able to possess.

In our present day, God is challenging the church to conquer spiritual powers that even the early church was not able to dispossess. Will the church rise to this challenge of faith and please our God by believing that He is great enough and powerful enough to subdue all things in heaven and earth under our feet (Rom. 16:20)? Will we be equal to this task? Will you?

For as in Adam all die, so in Christ all will be made alive. But each in his own turn: Christ, the firstfruits; then, when he comes, those who belong to him. Then the end will come, when he hands over the kingdom to God the Father after he has destroyed all dominion, authority and power. For he must reign until he has put all his enemies under his feet. The last enemy to be destroyed is death. For He "has put everything under his feet." (1 Cor. 15:22–27 NIV)

For from him and through him and to him are all things. To him be the glory forever! Amen. (Rom. 11:36 NIV)

References

Bready, John Wesley. 1946. *This Freedom—Whence?* New York: American Tract Society.

Curnock, Nehemiah, ed. 1909. *The Journal of John Wesley*. Vol. 1. London: Culley.

Ewart, Frank J. 1947. *The Phenomenon of Pentecost*. Houston: Herald.

Fischer, David, and Stephen Griffing. 1985. *The Worship of the Psalms in the Twentieth-Century Church*. Pasadena: Living Word Bible College.

Greenfield, John. 1931. *Power from on High*. London: Marshall, Morgan & Scott.

Nestle, Eberhard. 1960. *Novum Testamentum Graece*. Stuttgart: Privilegierte Wurttembergische Bibelanstatt.

Parker, Percy Livingstone, ed. 1974. *The Journal of John Wesley*. Chicago: Moody.

Richardson, Cyril, ed. 1970. *Early Christian Fathers*. New York: Macmillan.

Whiston, William, trans. 1974. *The Works of Flavius Josephus*. Vol 2. Grand Rapids: Baker.

About this book

David Fischer is a trusted leader, full of wisdom, with much to teach us all.
—John Dawson, founder, International Reconciliation Coalition, member of Youth with a Mission Global Leadership Team.

After carefully reading this manuscript, I believe it is one of the very best books on the subject of worship in print today. This book is not for the casual reader, but rather it searches out deep and heretofore hidden truths that reveal the full scope of worship as it involves both time and the eternal. Obviously, Pastor Fischer has penned this book under an unusually profound anointing. I strongly advise the reader to ask for eyes "anointed with eyesalve" in order to glean the best from it.
—Dr. Charlotte Baker, pioneer pastor and teacher in the ministry of the arts in worship and praise.

This is an incredible book! David Fischer opens our eyes to the reality of the connection of heaven and earth through worship. This book will give you a fresh passion and intimacy for God.
—Cindy Jacobs, co-founder, Generals of Intercession.

What David Fischer has done is to construct a comprehensive prophetic framework in which to understand how heaven and earth converge. This book pulsates with the throb of God's heart to manifest His glory through His people and demonstrate His Kingdom through His church.
—Steven Fry, founder, Messenger International, composer of *Thy Kingdom Come, Storyteller,* and other musicals.

About the author...

Dr. David Fischer is the Senior Pastor of Living Waters Christian Fellowship in Pasadena, California. Bible teacher, leader of prophetic worship, and pastor for twenty-seven years, he is a graduate of Stanford University and has studied both at Fuller and Princeton Theological Seminaries. President of Living Word Bible College and founder of Living Word Institute of Worship, Dr. Fischer also serves as an international coordinator of worship conferences. His ministry has taken him to sixteen nations on four continents. Father to Paul, Julie, and Karen, David Fischer resides with his wife Elaine in Pasadena, California.